FE Lecturer's Survival Guide

The Essential FE Toolkit Series

Books for Lecturers

Teaching the FE Curriculum – Mark Weyers

e-Learning in FE – John Whalley, Theresa Welch and Lee Williamson

FE Lecturer's Survival Guide – Angela Steward

FE Lecturer s Guide to Diversity and Inclusion – Anne-Marie Wright, Sue Colquhoun, Sina Abdi-Jama, Jane Speare and Tracey Partridge.

How to Manage Stress in FE – Elizabeth Hartney

Guide to Teaching 14–19 – James Ogunleye

Ultimate FE Lecturer's Handbook – Ros Clow and Trevor Dawn

A to Z of Teaching in FE – Angela Steward

Getting the Buggers Motivated in FE – Sue Wallace

Books for Managers

Everything You Need to Know about FE Policy – Yvonne Hillier

Middle Management in FE – Ann Briggs

Managing Higher Education in Colleges – Gareth Parry, Anne Thompson and Penny Blackie

Survival Guide for College Managers and Leaders – David Collins

Guide to Leadership and Governance in FE – Adrian Perry

Guide to Financial Management in FE – Julian Gravatt

Guide to Race Equality in FE – Beulah Ainley

Ultimate FE Leadership and Management Handbook – Jill Jameson and Ian McNay

A to Z for every Manager in FE – Susan Wallace and Jonathan Gravells

Guide to VET – Christopher Winch and Terry Hyland

FE Lecturer's Survival Guide

Angela Steward

continuum

Continuum International Publishing Group

The Tower Building   80 Maiden Lane, Suite 704
11 York Road   New York
London SE1 7NX   NY 10038

www.continuumbooks.com

British Library Cataloguing-in-Publication Data
A catalogue record for this book is available from the British Library.

ISBN: 0–8264–8550–2 (paperback)

Typeset by YHT Ltd, London
Printed and bound in Great Britain by Ashford Colour Press,
Gosport, Hampshire

Y0060833

Contents

For Dave

Acknowledgements

Special thanks to all my friends and colleagues in the FE sector who willingly shared their experiences of survival, and to Jill Jameson and Alexandra Webster, who generously shared their editorial experience.

Series foreword

THE ESSENTIAL FE TOOLKIT SERIES

Jill Jameson
Series Editor

In the autumn of 1974, a young woman newly arrived from Africa landed in Devon to embark on a new life in England. Having travelled half way round the world, she still longed for sunny Zimbabwe. Not sure what career to follow, she took a part-time job teaching EFL to Finnish students. Having enjoyed this, she studied thereafter for a PGCE at the University of Nottingham in Ted Wragg's Education Department. After teaching in secondary schools, she returned to university in Cambridge, and, after graduating, took a job in ILEA in 1984 in adult education. She loved it: there was something about adult education that woke her up, made her feel fully alive, newly aware of all the lifelong learning journeys being followed by so many students and staff around her. The adult community centre she worked in was a joyful place for diverse multi-ethnic communities. Everyone was cared for, including 90-year-olds in wheelchairs, toddlers in the crèche, ESOL refugees, city accountants in business suits and university level graphic design students. In her eyes, the centre was an educational ideal, a remarkable place in which, gradually, everyone was helped to learn to be who they wanted to be. This was the Chequer Centre, Finsbury, EC1, the 'red house', as her daughter saw it, toddling in from the crèche. And so began the story of a long interest in further education that was to last for many years . . . why, if they did such good work for so many, were Further Education (FE) centres so under-funded and unrecognized, so under-appreciated?

It is with delight that, 32 years after the above story began, I write the Foreword to *The Essential FE Toolkit*, Continuum's new series of 24 books on further education (FE) for teachers and college leaders. The idea behind the *Toolkit* is to provide a comprehensive guide to FE in a series of compact, readable books. The suite of 24 individual books are gathered together to provide the practitioner with an overall FE toolkit in specialist, fact-filled volumes designed to be easily accessible, written by experts with significant knowledge and experience in their individual fields. All of the authors have in-depth understanding of further education. But, 'Why is further education important? Why does it merit a whole series to be written about it?' you may ask.

At the Association of Colleges Annual Conference in 2005, in a humorous speech to college principals, John Brennan said that, whereas in 1995 FE was a 'political backwater', by 2005 it had become 'mainstream'. John recalled that since 1995 there had been '36 separate Government or Government-sponsored reports or white papers specifically devoted to the post-16 sector'. In our recent regional research report (2006) for the Learning and Skills Development Agency, my co-author Yvonne Hillier and I noted that it was no longer 'raining policy' in FE, as we had described earlier (Jameson and Hillier, 2003): there is now a torrent of new initiatives. We thought in 2003 that an umbrella would suffice to protect you. We'd now recommend buying a boat to navigate these choppy waters, as it looks as if John Brennan's 'mainstream' FE, combined with a tidal wave of government policies, will soon lead to a flood of new interest in the sector, rather than end anytime soon.

There are good reasons for all this Government attention on further education. In 2004/2005, student numbers in LSC-funded FE increased to 4.2m, total college income was around £6.1 billion, and the average college had an annual turnover of £15m. FE has rapidly increased in national significance regarding the need for ever greater achievements in UK education and skills training for millions of learners, providing qualifications and workforce training to feed a UK national economy hungrily in competition with other OECD nations. The 120 recommendations of the Foster Review (2005) therefore in the main encourage colleges to focus their work on vocational skills, social inclusion and achieving academic progress. This series is here to consider all three of these areas and more.

The series is written for teaching practitioners, leaders and managers in the 572 FE/LSC-funded institutions in the UK, including FE colleges, adult education and sixth form institutions, prison education departments, training and workforce development units, local education authorities and community agencies. The series is also written for PGCE/Cert Ed/City & Guilds Initial and continuing professional development (CPD) teacher trainees in universities in the UK, USA, Canada, Australia, New Zealand and beyond. It will also be of interest to staff in the 600 Jobcentre Plus providers in the UK, and to many private training organizations. All may find this series of use and interest in learning about FE educational practice in the 24 different areas of these specialist books from experts in the field.

Our use of this somewhat fuzzy term 'practitioners' includes staff in the FE/LSC-funded sector who engage in professional practice in governance, leadership, management, teaching, training, financial and administration services, student support services, ICT and MIS technical support, librarianship, learning resources, marketing, research and development, nursery and crèche services, community and business support, transport and estates management. It is also intended to include staff in a host of other FE services including work-related training, catering, outreach and specialist health, diagnostic additional learning support, pastoral and religious support for students. Updating staff in professional practice is critically important at a time of such continuing radical, policy-driven change, and we are pleased to contribute to this nationally and internationally.

We are also privileged to have an exceptional range of authors writing for the series. Many of our series authors are renowned for their work in further education, having worked in the sector for 30 years or more. Some have received OBE or CBE honours, professorships, fellowships and awards for contributions they have made to further education. All have demonstrated a commitment to FE that makes their books come alive with a kind of wise guidance for the reader. Sometimes this is tinged with world-weariness, sometimes with sympathy, humour or excitement. Sometimes the books are just plain clever or a fascinating read, to guide practitioners of the future who will read these works. Together, the books make up a considerable portfolio of assets for you to take with you through your journeys in further education. We hope the experience of reading the books will be interesting, instructive and pleasurable and that experience gained from them will last, renewed, for many seasons.

It has been wonderful to work with all of the authors and with Continuum's UK Education Publisher, Alexandra Webster, on this series. The exhilarating opportunity of developing such a comprehensive toolkit of books probably comes once in a lifetime, if at all. I am privileged to have had this rare opportunity, and I thank the publishers, authors and other contributors to the series for making these books come to life with their fantastic contributions to FE.

Dr Jill Jameson
Series Editor
March, 2006

Series Introduction

FE Lecturers' Survival Guide – Angela Steward

When I first proposed a book series on FE in 2003–4 to Alexandra Webster, publisher at Continuum in London, the first book on the list was a new 'Survival Guide for Lecturers in FE'. I thought this book was so important that, for me, it was the lynchpin of the new series. In my view, this was to be a book combining practical insights about the real situation facing lecturers in FE/ACL/LSC-funded/training and other PCET institutions every day, with in-depth research findings from the sector, advice and guidance, humorous, sensitive perceptions about FE and references to a range of further resources to bring much-needed relief to many beleaguered colleagues across the sector.

In other words, I wanted a book that would genuinely help lecturers survive and thrive through the difficult times and challenges facing a sector that Sir Andrew Foster has described as 'the neglected middle child' of UK education provision (Foster, 2005).

I am therefore absolutely delighted to commend to you this brilliant book written by Angela Steward – the *FE Lecturer's Survival Guide*. Angela has in-depth experience from many years in further education at the (literal!) chalk-face as a lecturer. Angela describes the context in which FE lecturers work, explaining why a survival guide is necessary. She advises us on the effective management of workloads in further education, suggests ways of making the most of our talents and skills in the ever-changing environment of FE, describes how to develop positive relationships with colleagues and students and explains how to create effective learning environments. Angela argues that it is the way that you interpret your role as a lecturer that makes the difference in survival terms. She advises us to develop clarity of purpose about why we work in FE, reflecting on ways to respond to the future by creating our own vision of this, using techniques to empower us and enable us to be more comfortable with change. Throughout the book, Angela provides us with original findings from her research with FE colleagues, with 'food for thought' examples and practical techniques to develop best practice for more effective and happier personal survival as an FE lecturer, even in the most difficult of circumstances.

Angela has 'been there, done it, got the T-shirt' from her own many years of experience in FE lecturing and extensive research carried out with FE lecturers. She really does understand the over-worked, over-stressed nature of the job, the non-stop challenges, demanding workloads, tough constraints and career insecurities faced by lecturers dealing with difficult students and staff daily. Her in-depth toolkit for survival provides an outstandingly helpful book for lecturers, team leaders, teachers, tutors and trainers in further education. It is everything that I hoped it would be when first proposing the series. I recommend to you this survival guide as an essential text for all lecturers and academic-related support and management staff in the learning and skills sector.

Dr Jill Jameson
Director of Research
School of Education and Training
University of Greenwich
j.jameson@gre.ac.uk

Introduction

Introducing the *Survival Guide*

What do you have to do to survive as an FE lecturer? What a question! The more you ask it, the more you realize that FE lecturers employ many different strategies to survive in college.

A popular image of a survivor is of someone who just manages to cling on to life despite the odds stacked against them. For many FE lecturers, surviving in college feels very much like that. The effort of clinging on, in what they often perceive as a hostile environment, takes up all their energy and results in tiredness, or even exhaustion. Perhaps preparation for lessons or workshop sessions does not get done satisfactorily. It may be that concentration lapses during teaching sessions, activities are mistimed or explanations muddled, and so students respond negatively. Constant interruptions and conflicting demands outside class might mean that marking and administration pile up.

Does all this sound familiar? If you feel like that you are not on your own. At times we may all have to work under pressure. Every job has its own stressful aspects. For FE lecturers, the beginning of the academic year brings new students, extra courses, different colleagues and changed systems, and is a time when perhaps it is quite usual to feel pressure, as everything seems unfamiliar. However, if the pressure becomes too much, or is too prolonged, it may result in stress. Of course, we all need a certain amount of stress to motivate us and to meet the challenges any job presents, but *too much stress* is what is of concern. There is an acknowledgement that stress exists in most college environments (AoC, 2002), but others take a somewhat controversial position and argue that the increased workload and stress associated with change can be attributed in part to the ways in which individuals organize themselves (Timperley and Robinson, 2000). Whether you agree with one point of view or the other, it is important for you to alleviate work-related pressure for the sake of your own well-being and professional development.

Everyone has a different way of coping with too much stress and, realistically, if you are an FE lecturer, the survival skills you need are developed as you work in a college and face the demands of your day-to-day workload. However, all too often you face problems or deal with events and it is only afterwards, perhaps when you are sharing your concerns or recounting a stressful incident, that a colleague says something like 'This works for me' or 'Why didn't you do so-and-so?' Of course, you keep this advice in mind to help you in the future – but it would have been really useful to have known it *before the event*!

Individual FE lecturers would define what stress means for them quite differently. It is only when working outside your 'comfort zone' that stress occurs, for example when you encounter new tasks or student groups you are not accustomed to, which makes you feel anxious or uncomfortable.

The FE Lecturer's Survival Guide provides advice about how to tackle workplace problems you may encounter now and in the future. The book is based on my experience as an FE lecturer, and upon experiences working with student-lecturers on Initial Teacher Education courses and with FE lecturers on in-service courses such as MA in Learning and Teaching. I draw on my research on FE lecturers' work to introduce you to constructive ways of thinking and working – rather than just surviving by cutting corners and making professional compromises to get by. In my view, being an FE lecturer should not just be about 'clinging on', but also about finding it a rewarding profession.

The FE Lecturer's Survival Guide promotes the image of a survivor as someone who has the energy, enthusiasm, drive and vitality to take a constructive view of supporting students' learning, and who is determined to make a success of their own role in achieving this.

The book is just as much for you if you are starting out in the sector, undergoing initial teacher education, or are an experienced lecturer. Even if you differ in your ability to cope at various times, all of you are confronting the demands that working in a college makes on you on a daily basis. The *Guide* provides features that a busy FE lecturer can browse through when needing ideas about how to cope with everyday pressures:

- 'Checkout and Workout' is an opportunity to identify your workplace concerns and follow this up with planning practical solutions to deal with them.

- 'Potential Pitfalls' are case studies illustrating FE lecturers' first-hand experiences of work-related pressures and problems. Their purpose is to make you aware of the pitfalls you may fall into so that you are forewarned. Obviously, for anonymity, lecturers' names have been changed – but the account is their own.

- 'Lecturers' Survival Strategies' are practical ideas and advice about overcoming everyday problems encountered in college. They provide examples from FE lecturers about the successful strategies and tactics they use to survive in college.

- 'Useful Ideas' are offered to encourage you to be positive in dealing with aspects of your job that you find stressful. They are commonsense ideas for developing your practice.

- 'Food For Thought' should help you think more about your own response to work-related problems and learn from workplace experiences – whether good or bad. 'Food for Thought' also provides an opportunity to deliberate about and reflect on your educational values and how best to realize them in practice.

My own research indicates that lecturers who are the most successful at surviving in FE display particular attributes and work in ways that we can all learn from (Steward, 2003). These successful ways of working form the content of the main chapters of the *Guide*.

- *Chapter 1 – Surviving in FE –* describes the context in which FE lecturers work and clearly sets out why FE lecturers need a *Survival Guide.*

- *Chapter 2 – Managing workloads effectively –* addresses ways of organizing time and dealing with people.

- *Chapter 3 – Using workplace experience constructively –* suggests ways of making the most of your talents in a changing environment.

- *Chapter 4 – Developing positive relationships –* provides examples of ways of working with colleagues and students effectively.

- *Chapter 5 – Creating a learning environment –* looks at classroom challenges, resource issues and new curricula requirements.

- *Chapter 6 – Interpreting your role –* argues that it is the way you interpret your role that is critical for survival.

1 Surviving in FE

Challenges faced by FE lecturers

It is now quite usual to hear FE lecturers expressing concern about the conditions faced by those working in colleges. If you listen to their concerns, many provide examples which imply that it is largely attempts to modernize and increase the effectiveness of colleges that have created or contributed to these conditions. Adjusting to a series of modernizing initiatives over recent years has presented a challenge for FE lecturers. For many of them, it seems as if nearly every aspect of their working life has either changed, or is about to change, in one way or another. Common sense tells us that change is an inescapable part of modern life. Therefore, to ensure its survival and future success, an FE college must adapt to the external demands placed on it. If FE lecturers perceived real advantages to change – for example better pay and working conditions – they might not put up any resistance. However, when change is perceived by many FE lecturers as a non-stop round of upheaval and job losses, and when they are confronted by consequences of change such as more demanding workloads, increased surveillance, tough financial constraints and insecurity of tenure, it is not surprising that many express their frustration, and that there is uncertainty about the future.

Challenges come from several quarters. First, from the Learning and Skills Council (LSC), which was set up by the government to modernize and simplify arrangements for the planning, funding and delivery of education and training for over–16s in England, except for higher education (HE). FE colleges are key providers of such provision in the Learning and Skills sector. The specific tasks of the LSC are to raise participation and attainment in learning by young people between 16 and 18 years of age, and to increase the demand for learning by adults. Modernizing strategies, such as those to raise skills levels for national competitiveness, improve the quality of education and training delivery and improve the sector's effectiveness and efficiency, mean that the conditions under which FE colleges are organized are shifting. These changing conditions mean lecturers' work is increasingly challenging.

The LSC has been stepping up the pace of change since its inception at the start of the new millennium, as it works to transform the Learning and Skills sector. So, teaching and learning, especially in vocational courses, are influenced by external factors such as structures and practices from outside as well as inside the college, and over which the college and lecturers have little control. Indeed, it is the stated mission of the LSC to put employers in the 'driving seat' and for colleges to put employers' priorities at the heart of what they do. As an FE lecturer, you are 'becoming a manager of a learning culture, much of which is not of your own direct making, as you respond to changing circumstances to preserve and hopefully improve the quality of learning, or to minimise the effects of external pressures' (Hodkinson and James, 2003). The lack of influence that some FE lecturers perceive is shaped by their belief that external factors – not teaching and learning – drive change. Such factors mean a changed ethos with loss of individual control and greater management control over core aspects of their work. How you collaborate with these factors is a question of professional judgement – which for lecturers may be a source of tension as they juggle with competing demands.

For more than a decade, since incorporation in 1993, the FE sector in England has experienced a period of rapid change (Gleeson, 2005). FE colleges are now very different places from those in which many FE lecturers were first employed and where established ways of working had been developed over time. Some FE lecturers may not find it easy to change as rapidly as the LSC would like, and even newly qualified FE lecturers may find the pace of change demanding. But the answer to these challenges is not to be found by reflecting back on easier times! Those days will not return and you have to recognize the changing nature of the FE sector and look to the future.

Although these modernizing strategies have been introduced with the genuine intention of equalizing opportunities for young people and adults through better access to learning, the reality is that FE colleges are in competition for students with other colleges, schools, sixth-form colleges and private and voluntary training providers in the same locality. FE colleges always had to attract business in the form of students, but marketing activity has to be increased, as funding is linked to the numbers participating as well as to the achievement of students. However, there is a substantial funding gap between the amount received by FE colleges and school sixth forms for comparative courses. The government acknowledges this gap and pledges to reduce it, but warns that continuing progress on narrowing the gap will not be easy and will depend on resources available. This is a point of view the LSC confirms when they say that it is clear the public purse won't stretch to pay for everything the government wants us to do and every-thing colleges and other training providers know they have to do to serve the needs of their communities (LSC, 2005). There are complex technical reasons for the funding gap, but the LSC's response to this challenging funding environment is to accelerate the rate of change across the sector. There has to be accountability for public money, but, as each FE college is a separate entity, funding decisions may reduce the quality of provision in some institutions. Nevertheless, FE lecturers are routinely expected to improve standards of teaching and learning. It appears that for some years the FE sector will be forced to provide quality education on the cheap.

A second source of considerable change has arisen from the government's *Education and Skills 14–19* White Paper (DfES, 2005). The White Paper was a response to the challenge issued in the report from the *Working Group on 14–19 Reform* (DfES, 2004) the previous year about how to fulfil the needs and aspirations of every young person. It is the reform outlined for National Curriculum Key Stage 4 (KS4) for young people aged 14 to 16 years that will have particular impact on FE colleges. Greater flexibility in the curriculum will ensure that young people are given a place to study at another school, an FE college or workplace for at least some of the time. Until the age of 16, young people will remain on the school roll but may spend up to two days a week in other settings. There are plans to make more places of study available that are much more tailored to the talents of individual young people, with greater choice about what and where to study and when to take qualifications. Reducing the prescriptive nature of the KS4 curriculum, and providing better qualification routes, makes it easier to combine academic and vocational learning. Indeed, under previous initiatives, there has already been a significant increase in the number of school pupils studying in different learning settings (Jephcote and Abbot, 2005). FE lecturers will increasingly be teaching younger students who undertake vocational education in an FE college for part of the school week. Although you may wholeheartedly agree with the government's vision of these changes as steps towards a more prosperous and fairer society, teaching a younger age group and remotivating disengaged learners brings new challenges for FE lecturers whose training and experience is with students aged 16 to 18 years and with adults. The majority of FE students are adults, but younger students are increasingly studying in an FE college.

The government's aim of expanding participation in higher education is a third source of immense change and challenge for FE colleges. The White Paper *The Future of Higher Education* (DfES, 2003) sets out plans for radical reform and investment in higher education, and the government's target is that 50 per cent of 18 to 30-year-olds will have a higher education experience by 2010, from a current level of about 44 per cent. This represents an enormous number of students – far too many for universities to cope with (Fiddy, 2004). It is clear, and indeed the White Paper makes it explicit, that much of this higher education experience will take place in an FE setting. It is also clear that one of the main vehicles to carry this forward will be the Foundation degree.

The government recognizes that the economy will increasingly need people with higher-level skills in future. The nature of jobs is changing as the economy becomes more knowledge-based and people in the UK are increasingly making their living through selling high-value services rather than physical goods. These trends demand a more skilled workforce with higher-level qualifications – but the government does not see these as being traditional three-year Honours degrees. As the increase in qualifications is connected with associate professional and high-level technician jobs (and this is where the skills gap is most acute), they seek expansion of higher education through work-focused Foundation degrees. These degrees are intended not only to match the needs of the economy, but also the demands of students themselves in the style of their delivery. The popularity of the two-year Foundation degree is increasing, and FE colleges are well-placed to offer flexible provision through supporting part-time degrees with a work-focused curriculum. Foundation degrees are a crucial link in the qualification progression route and can be topped up to an Honours degree with added study. All of this means that the qualification level an FE lecturer could be asked to work at is becoming even broader – from entry level to graduate or even postgraduate level. This is a challenge that those teaching in schools, sixth form colleges and universities do not have to contend with.

Lecturers in FE colleges work collaboratively with schools delivering the 14 to 19 agenda and with universities delivering higher education, and FE lecturers often undertake the same types of work as their school and university colleagues. Yet teachers in schools and lecturers in universities earn higher salaries than those teaching in the Learning and Skills sector, and salary levels achieved in the professional or vocational world cannot be matched by the majority of colleges. This raises the issue of equal pay for work of equal value. If lecturers had equal status with their colleagues in other sectors, this would be recognition of their efforts and their learners' achievements, and as a consequence, it would prove to be a morale-raiser. However, not all FE colleges have sufficient funding to enable them to implement fully the pay awards – another factor that contributes to many FE lecturers feeling undervalued. The salary system does not appear to reward the value of cooperation in collaborative schemes: it is not mutually beneficial.

FE colleges and lecturers are measured against models of quality provision through the process of regular performance reviews together with the outcomes of rigorous inspection regimes, conducted by the Office for Standards in Education (Ofsted) and the Adult Learning Institute (ALI). The LSC has agreed with colleges (and other training providers) an *agenda for change* to help them improve quality and respond better to employers' needs. The LSC states that: 'We'll get increasingly tough with those who don't deliver' (LSC, 2005). The LSC's threat means that the challenges look set to continue, even though it could be argued that within increased surveillance of FE lecturers' work lies a genuine interest in improving teaching and learning. Much of what FE lecturers do lies outside the direct scope of inspection, such as their commitment, care and 'going the extra mile' for students. Gleeson (2005) describes this as 'underground working', that is, doing lots of things over and above their job description. This is what FE lecturers often feel brings quality to their work in college and enhances the students' learning experience. However, this kind of support mostly goes unnoticed or is not officially recognized by college managers and inspectors.

It is clear that the conditions which challenge FE lecturers are varied and continuing. An FE college is a demanding environment in which to work, and how much individual input FE lecturers have in the way they do their work is diminishing. If an indication of support for the sector is consistently high levels of funding and pay, then support appears inadequate. All these factors are potential sources of stress for FE lecturers. However, they are not all new, and not just restricted to working in a college. Handy (2005) identifies five organizational situations that are likely to create stress for the individual.

Source of stress	Examples
Responsibility for the work of others	Overlapping or conflicting objectives
Innovative functions	Conflict between routine and creative aspects of the job
Integrative or boundary functions	Coordination roles, links with outside contacts, lack of control over others' demands
Relationship problems	Difficulties with boss or colleagues or the need to work with other people
Career uncertainty	Future career prospects doubtful, which affects the whole of a person's work

These five major sources of stress that create role problems in the workplace will be addressed in different chapters in this *Survival Guide*. Do you recognize any of the organizational situations that Handy identified across workplaces in your college?

The nature of stress is complex, but it can be identified as the adverse reaction people have to *excessive* pressures or other types of demand placed on them. The Health and Safety Executive identifies that: 'There is a clear distinction between pressure, which can create a "buzz" and be a motivating factor, and stress, which can occur when this pressure becomes excessive' (HSE, 2005:1).

Employers have a duty to ensure that risks arising from work activity are properly controlled. Use the following checklist to see how you and your college shape up.

CHECKOUT AND WORKOUT

The following items have been identified as sources of stress
by FE lecturers. Are any of these *excessive* for you at the
moment?

1 The amount of time spent on work-related
tasks outside college   Yes/No
2 The number of conflicts because colleagues
are under pressure   Yes/No
3 The amount of cover expected for staff
absences   Yes/No
4 The number of meetings at lunchtimes or
after work   Yes/No
5 The development of new courses and
resources   Yes/No
6 The amount of work there is to get through
each week   Yes/No
7 The different levels of ability within one class   Yes/No
8 The amount of preparation required for
inspection   Yes/No
9 The level of record-keeping for tracking
student achievement   Yes/No
10 The amount of responsibility for the level of
pay   Yes/No

If you have answered 'Yes' to more than five of the statements
because you find the item *excessive*, then you have identified
concerns about surviving in FE. This *Guide* may provide ideas
to help you understand and handle excessive stress. (Note – see
also the specialist *Essential FE Toolkit* book, *How to Manage
Stress in FE*, by Elizabeth Hartney, which contains more
detailed information on the identification and assessment of
stress.)

Statements 1 to 4 are potential sources of stress you can *try* to
control – so work out ways in which this is possible. Think
about perhaps developing your negotiating skills or planning
your diary more carefully. Ways of doing this are developed in
Chapter 2, where steps to consider before and during

negotiation are outlined and simple ways of managing your workload effectively are discussed.

Statements 5 to 7 require powers of organization to avoid stress. Perhaps think about using non-teaching time more purposefully, or be creative about lesson-planning. Ideas for organizing your time are also included in Chapter 2, and Chapter 5 has some ideas about planning and organizing sessions.

Statements 8 to 10 are demands of the system – so maybe you will have to learn to accept them and come to terms with them if you want to survive. Perhaps think about why record-keeping and inspection are important from *your students' perspective* – rather than yours.

Coping with stress in the workplace appears to be dependent upon two key factors:

- identifying potential stressors;
- the ability to take action to overcome them.

So, whatever the potential sources of stress at work you have identified as excessive for you, it is clear that to alleviate them you must begin by changing yourself. This is not easy, and there is no quick fix. It involves a commitment to do things differently – even if you are convinced the sources of stress are of the college's making.

Increasing burdens on FE lecturers

If you asked 100 FE lecturers in the Learning and Skills sector what a lecturer's job entailed and what they did on a typical day, you would probably get almost 100 different answers, due to the diversity of the sector and the constantly changing nature of what is happening in colleges and how they are run. There are over 400 FE colleges in England and Wales, which cater for a wide range of students and offer learning opportunities in vocational education for school students between 14 and 16 years, and post–16 education for school leavers and adults. Of the six million learners participating in education and training post–16, FE colleges serve about three million. FE colleges offer a huge selection of subjects, types of courses and academic and vocational qualifications at different levels: from basic skills needed for life through to professional qualifications and higher education degrees.

All this means that a lecturer's professional practice carries a variety of meanings and you would probably not get the same reply to your question about what an FE lecturer's job entailed from someone working with, say, catering students and someone working with students of media studies. To fulfil the wide-ranging curriculum on offer, it is obvious that FE lecturers come from a variety of backgrounds with different qualifications and previous industrial or business experience: accountants, artists, beauticians, builders, chefs and childcare workers. You could probably carry on through the alphabet naming previous occupations. Diversity of provision is reflected in considerable college-to-college variation (Hodkinson and James, 2003). It is difficult to achieve a consensus about what FE lecturers might do on a typical day in college, as the diversity of tasks carried out by FE lecturers is huge (Clow, 2005).

However, you probably *would* get a consensus that, as jobs are changing, so extra work is expected of FE lecturers and they are getting busier. At the start of the new millennium, Avis *et al.* (2001:75) discovered that lecturers 'consistently worked over hours . . . and we gained a sense of an overburdened profession'. They referred to the identification of a number of elements surrounding work in the sector: less individual freedom in the way lecturers work, heavier workloads, more emphasis on completing paperwork and stress on quality assurance issues.

All these elements have contributed to an overworked and over-stressed profession. Coping with the general workload of being an FE lecturer is stressful due to the sheer intensity of the experience, for example the physical demands, the high level of uncertainty and the complexity of the thought process. FE lecturers deal with a series of mini-deadlines in the form of fragmented, unrelated tasks all vying for position in the day-to-day schedule (Kyriacou, 2000). No two days are the same and FE lecturers have to switch from one task to another as unexpected events continually occur, always having to get to know new students and learn new procedures. More change is inevitable as issues raised by the government's reform agenda have implications for the future role of FE colleges (DfES, 2005). Despite all this, there is on the one hand an assumption that lecturers working in the sector will make the necessary adjustments to their practice to accommodate such changes, and on the other hand that the quality of their work will improve over time just through gaining the experience of doing the job.

When your day-to-day workloads seem crushing, and concerns focus on how best to get through the day, improving the quality of your work may not be high on *your* agenda. Lecturers' identities have traditionally been bound up in the activities of teaching and in their subject knowledge, but core elements of their work are being eroded as additional non-teaching tasks are added to their workload. This erosion has resulted in many lecturers suffering from low morale.

An extract from an employment contract of a main grade lecturer in one of the largest FE colleges in England illustrates the range of duties a lecturer might be expected to undertake:

> Formal scheduled teaching, tutorials, student assessment, management of learning programmes and curriculum development, student admissions, educational guidance, counselling, preparation of learning materials and student assignments, marking student work, marking examinations, management and supervision of student visit programmes, research and other forms of scholarly activity, marketing activities, consultancy, leadership, supervision, administration and personal professional development. (Huddleston and Unwin, 2002: 13)

Despite the length of this list of duties, you can most probably add more from your own experience! What the list illuminates, however, is that FE lecturers' workloads involve more than just teaching. The expectations of the role – both in teaching and non-teaching – are changing, and tensions arise as new and different skills are required. Even if you take a view that an FE lecturer has a role beyond the classroom or workshop as an extended professional, that is someone with a perspective that extends *beyond* the immediate demands of teaching, there is a growing imbalance between teaching and non-teaching tasks.

Whatever the reasons for change, increasingly colleges are

not easy places to work in but ones in which individuals may suffer stress and strain because of misunderstandings and dis-agreements, and conflicts arising as priorities change. The diversity and complexity of the duties place increasing burdens on FE lecturers. Opportunities for reflection and discussion are limited in the hurly-burly of everyday college life, and FE lecturers are working in an atmosphere that makes you feel that you are running hard just to stand still (Peeke, 2000). It is all too easy to become bogged down with the day-to-day activities so that little time is left for deeper thoughts about practice, and sometimes FE lecturers are so overwhelmed they are only concerned about how best to survive (Hillier, 2005).

The following case study captures how one FE lecturer, Dave, feels about his work in college. Dave has taught business studies for about ten years and for him an FE college as a workplace is fraught with difficulties.

POTENTIAL PITFALLS

I do get a general anxiety about the amount of work there is to do. New students, new courses, different lesson plans. It's an uphill struggle. I think it is very difficult to work in a situation where you are aware that what you normally do in the course of your job is inadequate. There's no one who makes you feel good and there's no one who really understands the commitment you're making. We do have a very pressurized life because slowly more and more is expected of us. There is more admin, there is more record-keeping and more meetings. So yes, we are under a great deal of pressure. Certainly colleagues seem to be suffering from high stress levels. I've been there myself so I know. Because I was so tired last year it made me really sit back and think . . . because you're no good to anyone when you're like that. So it's fundamental how you organize yourself and how you cope – think what you can do and what you can't. There are times when I feel as though I'm on skates.

How does Dave's case study compare with your experience? Do you, too, get the feeling that you are on skates?

It is clear that not all FE lecturers find working in college as fraught as Dave does. Although he appears to be under pressure he is becoming aware that to cope he has to think of what he can and cannot do. Although at a very low ebb, Dave has identified his own ways to survive – if only just. While accepting that others may see changes in the Learning and Skills sector as inevitable, or even exciting, for Dave they are a source of troubling anxiety. A lowering of morale impacts directly on the way you view the nature of new tasks that increase your workload – and on the manner in which you perform them. Recognition by others of the role he plays in college, and of the amount of effort he puts into fulfilling that role, are important. Like Dave, most FE lecturers seek an understanding from managers of the pressures they experience.

You don't want to end up like Dave and feel you are letting everyone down, as: 'To give the people we work with con-fidence in us as professionals, we have to be secure and happy enough ourselves in our roles, and not anxious' (Bolton, 2001:36). Anxiety is the enemy of confidence and we have to recognize that, and learn to control it as best we can. Looking on the bright side may sound trite when you are anxious but, according to Argyle (2001), it looks as if happiness is to a large extent in the mind, that is it depends on how we perceive things. The following examples illustrate three different per-ceptions and depict ways in which three FE lecturers manage to control their anxiety about workloads.

LECTURERS' SURVIVAL STRATEGIES

Share your concerns with colleagues you trust:

Remember, you're not on your own. We compare notes, compare strategies. It's all very informal. If students misbehave we'll say: 'What do you do about that?' 'What shall I do about that?' We provide one another with an uncritical way of saying you're doing all right – it's OK to find these students difficult. (Lecturer in Foundation Studies)

Negotiate blocks of non-teaching time:

For teaching sessions for two to three hours you really need a block of time to prepare, so the best timetable when you're full time is if you have non-teaching time together, say a morning or an afternoon. Then you can really get some work done. I try to get a timetable like that. (Lecturer in Engineering)

Find a quiet place to concentrate on tackling outstanding tasks:

When there's pressure to get marking or admin done, a strategy I use is to take time out, by leaving college early or coming in late, and working at home. That has worked very well. I probably get twice the work done as my staff room is not conducive to working in an organized way. (Lecturer in Management)

Thankfully, it is important to keep in mind that there are many FE lecturers for whom such survival strategies such as the three above are part of the toolkit of ideas and activities they employ day to day to work successfully. Are these strategies ones that might be applicable to alleviating your workplace burdens? Adopting strategies other FE lecturers use successfully may make a difference to your working life.

USEFUL IDEAS

- Slow down! You're not on skates. Take time to stop and think before you act.
- Get workplace problems out in the open. Don't pretend everything is fine if it isn't. Talk to someone you trust – out of college if necessary.
- Set aside specific times each week for important tasks such as curriculum or course development and lesson preparation. Be flexible and negotiate home-based working occasionally.
- To carry out the advice given in USEFUL IDEAS requires good communication and negotiating skills. How you improve and develop these skills is discussed in Chapters 3 and 4.

At the end of this chapter, in which challenges faced by FE

lecturers and the increasing burdens on them in college have been discussed, it is important to be aware that crises you may experience as an individual often reflect wider changes in education and in society (Brookfield, 1991). It is also important to remember that you can learn from both negative and positive experiences encountered in college. The following questions might be worth reflecting on to help you develop an awareness of the issues surrounding surviving in FE.

FOOD FOR THOUGHT

- Can you think of any situations when your confidence was shaken, and why?
- Can you think of any situations when you felt confident and acted confidently, and learn from them?

When you have identified the situations, reflect on why things went wrong and consider ways in which you can avoid getting into the same situation again. Then reflect on why things went well in one situation and on whether you could apply similar strategies in other situations in future.

---

2 Managing workloads effectively

Did you have a go at the 'Checkout and Workout' section in Chapter 1, inviting you to identify potential sources of excessive stress? If so, when you answered 'Yes' or 'No' to the statements and checked your responses, it became clear that potential sources of stress can be thought of in three ways. Sometimes they can be within your control to avoid. Sometimes they can be decreased by your powers of organization. Or thirdly, potential sources of stress may sometimes be systemic and beyond your individual control to change.

It is important to make a distinction between these three categories of potential stressors in order to manage your workload effectively. If you analyse and take control of this situation, you should be released to expend your time and energy on areas of your workload you can do something about and that you enjoy. That is not to say you just have to accept other stressful aspects of your workplace. Rather, it means you need to look at alternative ways of handling these things. Managing workloads effectively is dependent on identifying when things are getting too much for you and knowing what to do about the situation.

When Covey (2004) was describing the habits of highly effective people, he observed that striving for *efficiency* generally created problems and seldom resolved people's deepest concerns. If you are trying to resolve problems with your workload, it is worth bearing in mind that Covey considered being efficient was about 'things', whereas being *effective* was about 'people'. FE lecturers are often frustrated in their desires to be efficient. All you seem to do is meet more and more demands to be efficient. When you have met one target, another seems to be set. In popular terms, the goalposts always seem to be moving! Any frustration you may feel probably arises out of the expectations to be efficient that others place on you, for example the Learning and Skills Council's targets, the criteria of Ofsted and ALI, rather than those tasks you set yourself and consider important.

It is the tension between being efficient about things and being effective as a person that creates a need for *survival strategies*. Lecturers are as keen as college managers to improve student achievement, but from *their* perspective it is the quality of the educational process which students experience in college that brings added value: LSC targets or inspection criteria are not usually seen by lecturers as an end in themselves.

In this chapter, therefore, the focus will be on how dealing primarily with 'people' in college, that is students, colleagues and managers, will enable you to manage effectively the 'things' Covey described, such as the tasks that make up your workload.

Organizing timetables

Full-time lecturers in England and Wales are generally contracted to teach around 800 hours a year. Other lecturers may be contracted for a proportion of those hours, and part-time lecturers may be employed on a sessional basis. FE lecturers delivering higher education courses (for example Foundation degree courses) may be contracted to teach around 550 hours a year (plus preparation and marking). Whatever type of contract you have, it is usually just the teaching sessions and hours that are shown on your timetable for each week, term, semester or year.

An important first step for any FE lecturer considering ways of managing workloads effectively ought to be a review of their timetable. Timetables are the documents used to calculate hours and allocate classes. Lecturers' timetables identify subjects, the level of courses and the nature of the student group being taught. Timetables are everyday documents that structure individual and organizational life. In FE colleges, which regulate work through measurement against inspection criteria, national targets and teaching standards, timetables offer insight into FE lecturers' daily routines. However, as documents, timetables do little to reveal the pressures FE lecturers may be under, as they do not reveal all the hidden demands of the job, such as dealing with difficult groups or second marking a colleague's work.

Do you sometimes find you are working to the limits of your capacity? At times, many FE lecturers feel they have been thrown in at the deep end and are struggling to survive. It is not just if you are on a teaching placement for initial teacher education or when you start working for the first time in college that you may feel this. Experienced FE lecturers may also feel as if they are struggling to survive when they are asked to teach a new subject, course or entirely different group of students. It may be that your timetable has been changed at the last minute because of staffing difficulties, or as a part-timer you have agreed to teach a different class or course and accepted a contract to teach specific hours which the college found difficult to cover. When asked to teach things you have not taught before, for example covering for staff absence, not only is more preparation time required, but also your confidence may diminish as new situations challenge your assumptions, beliefs and understandings about yourself (Hanson, 1996). Is it a challenge you recognize? Is it a challenge you relished, or one that knocked your confidence?

First, the way timetables are constructed may actually contribute to your workload. What is visible on the timetable relates to your teaching commitments, as only the hours in the classroom are usually shown. What is invisible is what you have been timetabled for, which makes a difference to your workload: the number of students in the group, the level of work, whether it is new for you or the college, the number and type of assessments, the nature of the students and the availability of appropriate resources.

Second, timetables do not represent the totality of your workload. About a third of a full-time lecturer's hours in the working week is not accounted for on the timetable. A part-time or sessional lecturer is paid for teaching hours, but usually the contract states that a proportion of the hourly rate is for preparation and marking done outside class and for holiday pay. What appears to be problematic is what cannot be seen on the timetable: the administrative load, frequent meetings, increasing student demands, tight deadlines, constant curriculum change and continuous quality improvements. These factors, along with the way teaching is allocated and organized, hold hidden pressures and increase lecturer's workloads – which leads me to label them 'invisible workloads'.

What do I mean by 'invisible workloads'? From my own research, I found that college managers recognize that some timetables are less onerous than others (Steward, 2002). Some topics or subjects are considered 'easier' as they are less complex to teach and involve less marking and preparation. College managers acknowledge that different subjects and levels make different demands: that is, there is a difference between entry level, FE and HE teaching, and there is a difference between students' academic ability and motivation. However, time-tablers do not appear to take these factors into account, as the following example of an 'invisible workload' experienced by Christine, who is a part-time lecturer in mathematics and science, demonstrates.

POTENTIAL PITFALLS

Christine found that as a part-timer she has to work almost twice the hours she is contracted for if she is to carry out her job to meet the requirements of the college.

Last year the group I taught had 12 students in it. It was a new degree course, but this year I've got 21 in the group. I'm a part-timer and what I found difficult this year was the marking and tutorials. When you've got a 4,000-word project to mark it does take time – I reckon over an hour by the time you've read it, made your comments on the assignment, allocated a mark, word processed your feedback and added it to the results sheet. So say I spent 12 hours marking last year, for the same money I'm having to spend about 21 hours this year. It's the same for tutorials – last year I could just about fit a short tutorial for each student into a three-hour session – this year I can't. So I come in early and stay on after class – but if I didn't do it in my own time the quality would suffer because I'm paid for the minimum class contact time as it is.

This example of an 'invisible workload' experienced by Christine undoubtedly demonstrates that being aware of what is on your timetable is an important first step in managing your workload effectively. Christine's account reveals that a great deal of work carried out by FE lecturers is invisible in the system, in that it is done out of college in a lecturer's own time through goodwill, or not paid for. Timetables are a regular topic of conversation in college staff rooms and often a source of frustration. It is unlikely you will get your ideal timetable with all your favourite groups of students and subjects or parts of the curriculum that you particularly enjoy, but it might be worth trying to negotiate a more manageable one.

Part-time lecturers such as Christine do not usually have this option. There is a widely held notion that many lecturers do not work full time out of choice. While admittedly some full-time lecturers may choose to reduce their hours for personal or health reasons, most colleges employ part-time lecturers for the flexibility this offers. Working part time may or may not be out of choice and earning a living may mean taking whatever is on offer. As a part-time lecturer you may take on something new, or at awkward hours, just for the experience you need or to 'get your foot in the door'. Once you have *agreed* to develop new courses or work extra hours, do so with grace and not constant complaints. The time to deal with timetable requests is *before* you agree to them. There is a great deal of difference between feeling used by the college and using the college offer to gain experience. To achieve this, the skills of negotiation can be employed.

Therefore, knowing that the way timetables are constructed can contribute to your workload, can you identify what it would be important for you to negotiate about with your current timetable? Use the 'Checkout and Workout' task to help you with this.

CHECKOUT AND WORKOUT

The factors outlined below have been identified by FE lecturers as problematic in their timetables and may contribute to an 'invisible workload'. Your task is to:

1 Identify whether they appear on your timetable.
2 Decide whether they are acceptable.
3 Ask yourself whether they are worth negotiating about to enable you to manage your workload effectively.

Invisible factors on timetables	Identify	Accept	Negotiate
Teaching courses new to the college			
Teaching subjects completely new to you			
Travelling time to different sites			
Back-to-back sessions with no break			
Different levels consecutively			
No blocks of time free for preparation			
Recommended hours not allocated			
Combined groups, e.g. Years 1 and 2			
Uneven balance of hours over year			
Covering for absent colleagues			
Marking burden for large groups			
Notoriously difficult student group			

Can you identify anything else on your timetable that is *specific* to your subject or your college and that you would like to change through negotiation with the timetabler?

If there are items that you consider worth negotiating on, the following sequence of steps and ideas should help you prepare. Negotiation is about two people discussing an issue and reaching an agreement. Negotiation is not about competing but aiming for collaboration and finding common ground – and if necessary accepting a compromise. To be effective, focus on how you communicate with the timetabler.

USEFUL IDEAS

Effective negotiation

- Identify the specific problem.
- Identify your key concern(s).
- Try to envisage the problem not just from your point of view but (in this case) from the timetabler's point of view.
- Don't make it a personal issue between you and the timetabler, but consider it an organizational issue.
- Think of different ways that the problem could be resolved – have some answers ready.
- Decide before you start to negotiate what would be an acceptable solution for you.
- Remember that negotiation implies a two-way process – it should be mutually beneficial.
- Only after you have gone through all these steps, approach the timetabler to negotiate on any problems you wish to resolve.
- Don't see negotiation as a battle of wills and try to score points or air all your grievances.

Accept that you may not be able to achieve your ideal time-table. Remember that it is good to extend yourself sometimes by working in new areas. Negotiation skills are vital not only in trying to resolve timetable problems with your manager, but also for using with:

- students in tutorials;
- colleagues in team meetings;
- schoolteachers when collaborating about vocational courses;
- employers when arranging work placements;
- speakers when organizing visits.

FE lecturers who manage their workloads effectively are skilled at negotiation and try to deal with issues before they become problems. Communicating your frustrations to your manager in a professional way usually brings a resolution, whereas complaining to anyone and everyone in the staff room who will listen to you does not. More tips about communicating effectively are given in Chapter 3.

Work–life balance

Getting the right balance between home and work improves the situation both at work and at home – but the trouble is it is not easy to achieve. Anybody who sets out to redress the balance between work and home is seen by many managers as bad news for a college, as the assumption is that if you balance your time in a different way home 'wins' and gets more time, and work 'loses' and gets less. However, by linking work and home issues, people tend to become more effective and less stressed, as barriers and demarcations between work and home disappear (Rapoport, 1999). It is in working to achieve a better work–life balance that you can flourish rather than just survive.

It is interesting that FE colleges recognize changing work patterns in their potential student base and update courses by offering flexible attendance and introducing family friendly policies. Yet when it comes to experimenting with work methods for FE lecturers, both managers and lecturers still tend to see home and work as separate entities. There is a natural connection between a person's work life and all other aspects of life. As Senge (1990:307) lucidly explains: 'We live only one life, but for a long time organisations have operated as if this simple fact could be ignored, as if we had two separate lives.' I would advocate that blurring the boundaries between home and work is one way of managing your workload effectively.

The reality of college life is that lecturers' actions reveal that home and work are inextricably linked. You may hear colleagues say that they have come into college to escape the tensions at home. Alternatively, colleagues stay at home to avoid conflict or pressure at work, and ring in sick. Although these actions indicate the link, as lecturers make connections between work and home experiences, they are certainly not contributing to the work–life *balance* that enables lecturers to manage workloads more effectively.

CHECKOUT AND WORKOUT

Your answers to the following questions may help you assess whether you have got your work–life balance right.

1 Do you frequently arrive for teaching sessions unprepared?
2 Do you frequently apologize to students for not having marked their work?
3 Do you frequently keep students waiting or forget appointments with colleagues?
4 Do you frequently take college work home and still not do it?
5 Do you frequently get impatient with students who are difficult or aggressive?
6 Do you frequently find household chores are not done to your satisfaction?
7 Do you frequently grumble about work to friends or family?
8 Do you frequently find you cannot relax at weekends or are too tired to socialize?
9 Do you frequently have sleepless nights or wake up worrying about college problems?
10 Do you frequently get into arguments with family or friends about trivial things?

Going through the questions should raise your awareness of what's involved in trying to maintain a work–life balance. If you answered 'Yes' to any of the first five questions, then you are most likely experiencing pressure at work. If you answered 'Yes' to any of the last five questions, then it may be that workplace stress is having an effect on life outside work as you bring your work problems home. There is only a problem when there is a misfit between your work commitments and home commitments that disrupts your work–life balance.

At the risk of perpetuating a stereotype that might have been valid years ago, work–life balance is often viewed as unachievable because of the imbalance between men and women in terms of duties and responsibilities at home. Addressing ways of achieving an equitable division of domestic responsibilities is a critical first step in achieving a work–life balance for both partners and housemates. Your circumstances may mean that issues such as childcare, looking after relatives, food shopping, general cleaning, washing and ironing, time-consuming sports or hobbies and doing the garden or decorating need discussion. 'Useful Ideas on Effective Negotiation' on page 26 would come in very useful here! Living alone may bring different issues and pressures, as you cope with household chores and DIY single-handedly.

Too often, FE lecturers are not aware that their work performance is declining or their home life is suffering until fatigue becomes exhaustion and their ability to cope worsens. This may be a consequence of workplace events such as starting a new job, trouble with a colleague, demanding students or difficult working conditions. Or it may be as a consequence of personal sources of stress such as the death of someone close, serious illness in the family, relationship problems or even something like moving house. Reactions to stress vary and some of you will be able to take levels of stress for longer than others because of your personality type – but eventually your health will suffer if stress levels are sustained. Remember, there is only a problem when there is a misfit between your work commitments and home commitments.

FOOD FOR THOUGHT

How do you know when you are not managing your work–life balance effectively? Warning signs of stress manifest themselves in a range of symptoms that might be affecting your health, emotions or behaviour. To develop your awareness, reflect on whether you exhibit any of the warning signs given below.

Warning signs: health

Fatigue
Feeling dizzy
Feeling under the weather

Frequent coughs and colds
Headaches
High cholesterol
Hypertension
Stomach aches
Muscular tension, e.g. back pain

Warning signs: behaviour

Achieving less
Avoiding people
Becoming accident prone
Neglecting relationships
Neglecting your appearance
Not sleeping properly
Slow to respond
Smoking/drinking more
Working longer hours
Unable to relax

Warning signs: emotions

Aggression
Demotivated
High levels of anxiety
Indecisiveness
Irritability
Feeling a failure
Feeling hopeless
Lack of confidence
Loss of sense of humour
Low morale
Mood swings

When you reflect on the warning signs of stress identified above, you will notice that they could all potentially cross the boundaries between home and work. For example, not sleeping properly may mean you are slow to respond to problems at work and you become irritable with people at home. Not all the signs will necessarily be a problem for you, as people experience the symptoms and perceive stress in different ways. Your personality type affects your response, as does the level of support you already have.

The first step is recognizing the warning signs in yourself. If you do, don't ignore them and hope that they will go away. Don't pretend they're not there. However difficult it may seem, you must deal with them. You need to identify why the symptom occurs and when it occurs so that you can ultimately deal with the cause of the stress. Some suggested ways of dealing with the warning signs are provided:

- Visit your GP and discuss the symptoms, or take advice from a pharmacist.
- Don't suffer in silence – ring a helpline.
- Talk to friends and family.
- Talk to a colleague, manager or union representative.
- Talk to a member of your Human Resources Department or a counsellor.
- Check you have a healthy diet and ensure a regular sleep pattern.
- Set aside times for relaxing and socializing – don't work longer hours.

When I first started at college you used to have a lunch break and breaks morning and afternoon. You'd take a break and now you don't. Everybody just sits at their desk miserably hunched over working. (Lecturer in modern languages)

If you recognize yourself in the quote above, the time to take action is now. At work, taking short breaks for coffee or lunch with colleagues would be a good start. Don't feel guilty about leaving work promptly as you should not have to fight for the right to finish work on time. Start by making small changes at home and see what happens. If you don't take some action there is a danger of burning out. If you recognized a lot of the warning signs, think about taking time off, as this allows you to recharge your batteries.

You can make choices about work–life balance – and it may be that work is your priority. As long as you are honest about your commitments to those around you, then you can choose to do what is important to you. What works for other FE lecturers may not necessarily work for you – but the following strategies may be ones to consider and they may prove useful to you in maintaining a work–life balance.

LECTURERS' SURVIVAL STRATEGIES

Take care of your health and get things into perspective:

You need good health, lots of strength, lots of energy and also to keep a fairly level head and be able to see things clearly and not let your own emotions get in the way, because students do challenge, they do get upset and try to take things out on you. You have to be able to stand back and look at things from a detached point of view. I think that's really important. (Lecturer in hairdressing)

Switch off from work problems at home and take time to unwind:

I'm fortunate that in the evening I can switch off. If I do take some work home, if I've got something to plan, I'll do it immediately so that the rest of the evening is mine. Weekends are fine because one or other day I won't do any college work at all. Even if it's stacked up to do I'm not going to do it. It's normally a Sunday and we take the dogs over by the river or across the fields and I think that's important. (Lecturer in drama)

These illustrations of survival strategies that lecturers use are good examples of the way they cope with stressful lives. These lecturers are not immune to stress, but the pressures experienced are not debilitating. Perhaps the most significant thing you can learn from their successful strategies is that they have not only identified their stressors but also taken action to overcome them rather than worrying about them.

Investing time

It is fascinating how differently time can be perceived. It is not only that different people look at time in different ways, but also that time is interpreted differently in different contexts. As a phenomenon, time is a valuable but finite resource (Mullins, 1999). You cannot buy it, you cannot replace it, you can use it or waste it and everything you do requires it! Time can be manipulated. It can be a 'window of opportunity' for meeting important visitors to the college – however busy you are. Or it can be used as an excuse to get out of meeting the visitors if you are not really that interested. If you set aside an hour in your day to prepare a lesson, the time flies and you seem to have to pack up and go and teach almost as soon as you started the preparation. However, if you are taking a group of students to a trade exhibition, waiting for an hour for transport because of a mix-up in times seems interminably long. The hour just drags and you are annoyed and fed-up.

You can see that how you use your time is an important decision in managing your workload effectively. Otherwise, you are easily diverted into spending time on unimportant or trivial tasks and stretching them to fit the time available. Dealing with emails is probably a good example of this phenomenon, as you can flick through them if you are in a rush – or spend ages going through them if you are too tired to start on more important tasks.

It is all too easy to spend your time dealing with things which should have been done 'yesterday'. Your manager, a colleague or an administrator puts pressure on you to get the job done straightaway and then you panic, drop everything else and rush to do the job. Things start to feel out of your control, and this is because you are letting other people organize your life. It is not very satisfying, either, because when you do not deliver to agreed deadlines people get upset and annoyed. You don't get positive feedback either when you rush into the office with the completed registers after admin staff have had to hassle you to total them. You begin to get the feeling that nobody appreciates how hard you are working, and there's just not enough time in the day! Of course, there are 24 hours in the day for everyone.

But does it sometimes feel as if others seem to have more hours in the day than you? Perhaps you are wasting your time without realizing it. Have a go at the 'Checkout and Workout' to see if you are.

CHECKOUT AND WORKOUT

Timewasters are often about being disorganized and distracted. Check if you are guilty of any of the following:

1 Searching for lost examination papers among the clutter on your desk.
2 Hoarding old handouts and shuffling through them for your next lesson.
3 Losing lesson plans not filed in course folders and having to redo them.
4 Storing students' work somewhere and spending ages trying to find it.
5 Piling up marking for different groups haphazardly then having to sort it to hand back.
6 Being unable to find documents on the computer and rewriting them.
7 Arranging a tutorial when you are teaching and having to rebook it.
8 Mislaying notes of minutes and having to write them up from memory.
9 Rushing out of a meeting to telephone and cancel a clashing appointment.
10 Redoing a report a colleague prepared that is not up to your standard.

Are you guilty of any of these timewasters? If so, it is easy to see why you think there are not enough hours in the day. Work out how you could overcome some of these timewasters. What do you need to do to organize your day better?

It is difficult to change your habits – but the benefit of changing your ways is that you appear to have more time in the day. I'm sure you have seen someone in a flurry of activity trying to get things done in a panic at the last minute and felt a bit sorry for them. Constant activity is not necessarily effective. Don't let that person be you in the future – get organized!

There are simple steps you can take so that you don't forget to do jobs by the deadline. The easiest is probably to compile a 'To Do' list to remind you what needs to be done, and then cross if off as it's completed. If you spend a few minutes at the end of each working day jotting down jobs to do, and leave the list in a prominent position on your desk or notice board, then you can go home without worrying about them and the list is there to jog your memory when you return to work the next day. Take a few minutes when you arrive to review the list before getting embroiled in other jobs. You will feel a sense of accomplishment as you tick off the jobs when they're done.

Although a 'To Do' list is really useful, a problem with just relying on this way of managing your workload effectively is that it is possible to fill the day with the immediate jobs on the list and not think about important, long-term, time-consuming jobs such as planning a scheme of work for the next academic year. You find yourself just reacting to what is urgent, but if you plan ahead you can create your own workload.

Using a diary or calendar is essential for planning ahead. You can note important dates, for example term dates, an External Verifier's visit, examination dates, Open Days, etc. If you use the diary or calendar *methodically* to record future commitments, you will know where you are expected to be on certain dates and at what time. You will have a record of what you have agreed to. In this way, you won't forget meetings and will show up for appointments on time. The impression you give will then be of someone responsible and dependable – and organized. If you use a large diary with a 'day-to-a-page', you can write your reminders in it too. Whatever you use must be portable so you can carry it around and have it ready to consult when fixing appointments. Using the calendar on your computer may not be ideal – but treating yourself to an electronic personal organizer would be. Just remember to use only one device for your reminders and appointments, otherwise you will get into a muddle.

Use your diary or calendar to block out time for preparation and marking, especially at busy times when you are dealing with phase tests, summative assessments, project presentations or exhibitions of students' work. Treat these entries just as you do other appointments and if you're asked to do something else at the same time, keep the space clear by replying that your diary is full that day, before trying to fix a *mutually* convenient time. Don't be too rigid about this, but don't give up all your time either. It is about weighing up your priorities and getting the balance right. Don't book up every minute of the day: leave time for unexpected events and mishaps.

It is becoming clear that managing workloads effectively is really about managing yourself and the secret is that you must have a clear idea of what is important to you. My research has shown that successful FE lecturers appear to assess their workloads and identify what is worth investing their time in (Steward, 2004). This is a way of prioritizing tasks based on values. If you want to be successful, you need to focus on what is important to you and what you want to achieve. So don't spend all your time making lists and filling in your diary or organizing your calendar. Spending time on a curriculum development project is more exciting, particularly when it is in your specialist subject and you are going to be responsible for delivering the new course. To make time to undertake such a project means having to say 'No' to unimportant things so that you can say 'Yes' to things that are important to you and then invest your time in them. You may have to work harder before a deadline, but if it is your project, the burst of activity gives you a buzz and you get pleasure from achieving your goals.

If you think only of managing your workload from day to day, you miss out on important opportunities. Spending time wisely requires you to think ahead. Ask yourself: what do I want to achieve this academic year? Set yourself a couple of personal goals that are attainable. These goals may be determined by you or through negotiation with colleagues. Then think what tasks you need to do, term by term, to accomplish your personal goals, and immediately schedule time for them. Evaluate your workload each week – rather than daily – and in this way you will get a better picture of what is important to do, not just what is urgent.

Manage your workload effectively to the best of your ability – but don't feel guilty if you don't meet all your own personal goals or if you have to change your schedule. Try to ensure that your investment of time reflects Covey's (2004) theory that efficiency comes through organizing your time but effectiveness comes through dealing with people and focusing on results – as the following examples of survival strategies demonstrate.

LECTURERS' SURVIVAL STRATEGIES

Invest time in people and focus on relationships – with students in particular:

At the very beginning of this particular cohort they had an in-depth tutorial where I tried to build up a relationship with them so that I knew them as individuals, where they were coming from. This was done very early on and it took up a lot of time and it meant being here until late to actually do this. I did the whole thing geared to getting to know them as individuals. It helped me because I knew where they were coming from. (Lecturer in early years education)

Investing time by delegating tasks – especially to students – it is mutually beneficial:

To save my time I have got the students to work harder and to research their own practice and then bring those findings back to the group for discussion and further analysis. Researching their practice, and sharing their practice in class, has not only helped them develop their skills but also informed me, which helps when developing things for the future. (Lecturer in health and social care)

Invest time in preparing resources and reap the rewards later:

To try and make life a bit easier for me I may put a lot of time into initial preparation of certain activities because I know I can use those over and over again. An example of one thing I did for anatomy and physiology students was made a game for them to use where they had a bare skeleton and had to pick out correct names to label the bones, etc. Now that took a lot of time for me to make and have laminated, but I have used it over and over again. So subsequent lessons are much easier to plan and prepare. (Lecturer in health care)

In this chapter I have discussed the importance of managing your workload effectively. Although there are practical things that you can do, such as organizing your timetable, maintaining a work–life balance and investing your time in worthwhile activities, the critical thing that comes out of the discussion is that success comes from managing yourself. Use the following quote in 'Food for Thought' to help you reflect on this

FOOD FOR THOUGHT

In arguing that vocational education requires you not only to develop a *sense of how to be* in line with demands of the workplace, but also to develop *sensibility*, that is requisite feelings, morals and the capacity for emotional labour, Colley *et al.* (2003:478) quote excellent advice from Bourdieu, which is to create a 'meaningful world, a world endowed with sense and value, in which it is worth investing one's practice'.

3 Using workplace experience constructively

My purpose in this chapter is to help you think about your own response to workplace experience. When you start a new job as an FE lecturer, whether it is from an initial teacher education course, a job in industry or another college, it takes time to learn the college procedures, protocols and conventions. It also takes time to get to know the people in your curriculum area and build professional relationships with colleagues. However, once you have settled into the job, it is all too easy to get drawn into routines and ways of thinking that are not very positive or productive. If the atmosphere in your staffroom is negative and morale is generally low, it is difficult to do your work well and enjoy it, and almost impossible to be creative and put forward new ideas or overcome problems.

The way you respond to organizational systems, teaching commitments and work colleagues shapes the way you view yourself as an FE lecturer. Do you see workplace experience as problematic and a reflection on your inability to cope, or as a challenge that is part and parcel of being an FE lecturer? If the former, you are likely to end up struggling and dispirited, and will start to worry about how long you will be able to manage to stay in the job and whether all your effort is worth it. If the latter, you are more likely to remain positive, with developing confidence in your ability to find a solution to whatever problems you encounter in the workplace.

Are you someone whose first reaction is to 'keep your head down' when a new initiative is announced or curriculum changes are demanded – just in case you get roped in for more work? This may be an effective survival strategy in the short term if you feel overloaded or that you lack the skills required. However, one of the consequences of this is that you miss out on new projects and so pass up the opportunity of developing your knowledge and learning new skills that may be valuable for your professional development and future progression.

A more constructive survival strategy would be to look beyond your immediate workplace experience and try to understand why your college operates in the way it does, and to become more involved in college life. An awareness of the way your college functions as a workplace may help you to have more understanding of why budgets are fixed as they are, or why you have to provide statistics on students' attendance, retention or achievement. You will still have to stick within the budget when ordering new equipment or work out the figures required, but you might be more disposed to do the jobs – and with fewer moans and groans!

'Keeping your head down' may be a way of protecting yourself, but it is not an effective way of using your workplace experience constructively. Try to ignore the negative atmosphere, if there is one. Do your own teaching as well as you can and look for opportunities to get out of the situation. This does not necessarily mean changing jobs or asking for a transfer (although these could be options). It might mean keeping an eye open for special projects or professional development courses that make the best use of your abilities. Try to do something positive for yourself and discuss your options with your manager so that when the opportunity for better things arises you are ready to take it.

Sometimes the only barrier to positive action is yourself because you are prepared to accept things as they are – even if you are unhappy about the situation. There is usually something that can be done and a first step will be to look at the context in which FE lecturers work.

Understanding the college as a workplace

Different lecturers are motivated by different things. Some FE lecturers go to work only for the money; they do their work adequately but take no interest in the college beyond their immediate workload. As a lecturer, it is very easy to become isolated if you work on your own in the classroom or workshop. This may be a deliberate choice, or because you are a part-time lecturer, or perhaps you have been timetabled to work more in the evenings or at weekends when fewer people are around. Other lecturers are definitely interested in becoming more involved in college life. Whatever your position, if and when an opportunity arises to be involved in a project or new initiative in your college, make the most of it.

The reason this is a good survival strategy is that learning about your occupation as an FE lecturer occurs in the workplace through your *participation* with the people who work there (Lave and Wenger, 1991). As a newcomer to college, you learn about what is required of you from more experienced people as you become immersed in the college community as a member of staff. As you become engaged in your work in college, you become aware of how things are done, what is expected of you and how other people feel about their jobs. It is more than just keeping yourself informed of changes that affect your day-to-day workload. It is an acceptance of Bruner's (1997) theory that learning and thinking are always situated in a cultural setting, and always dependent upon the utilization of cultural sources. What this means is that to find out about your job, say when you are thinking about how to plan a course you have not taught before, you can learn by exchanging ideas with your colleagues in the department and across the college. Colleagues are key cultural sources of your learning. This involves asking them questions about what they do, observing how they do things and discussing problems. It may be technical problems such as how to get digital photographs into your handouts, how to change course material in electronic format into speech for a student with visual impairment, or how to book and use video-conferencing. Then again, it may be more complex processes such as risk assessment before a field trip, how to decide whether an HND team project is allocated a merit or distinction, or how to organize a real work environment effectively for NVQ students.

The following two cases illustrate how sharing problems about everyday workplace experiences and discussing them with colleagues who have more experience helps these lecturers think about the issues more constructively and learn how things are done in their department in their college.

LECTURERS' SURVIVAL STRATEGIES

Consult colleagues about what it is appropriate to do in problematic situations:

I talk to a particular colleague about a lot of things I do, how I organize myself and the decisions I make, or whatever. That's helped – especially in my work-based tutorials as well as handling students and getting the best out of a situation. She has helped me with getting stuff internally verified, with a problem I had and marking and so on. I'm very lucky because I'm in a department where staff are very supportive so I've always had someone I can turn to and make sure I'm doing it correctly. (Lecturer in hospitality and catering)

Engage in professional conversations with colleagues and learn how to fit in:

I would say that in our department the work climate is actually very good. I don't have any problems talking to colleagues and getting advice. The course team meetings are usually very constructive and the head of department is normally extremely supportive. I seem to have got a reasonable amount of respect from other people since I've been here – which is a way of saying you fit in, you're OK, patted on the back from time to time, which is quite nice. (Lecturer in electronics and telecommunications)

The disposition of these two lecturers is obviously important. Perhaps they had a natural tendency to ask questions and be communicative, or an inclination to be a team player. Your temperament obviously affects the way you feel about day-to-day problems: whether you deal with them or succumb to them and sink under the pressure. Learning about what is involved in becoming a lecturer and coping with problems that arise requires *activity* on the part of the lecturer. In the cases above, lecturers took action by:

- identifying where they needed help;
- seeking guidance about specific difficulties.

A key factor in these cases was that they both perceived their workplace as having a 'supportive' culture. The first case portrays a relaxed approach to learning about work through talking to a more experienced colleague. Chapter 4, 'Developing positive relationships,' provides a section on ways of working with colleagues that discusses the importance of building informal support networks.

The second case portrays a more structured approach to learning through attendance at course team meetings. Everyone gets involved in different sorts of meetings in college. They can range from a casual chat in the staff room to an organized meeting in your department. You might have one-to-one meetings with a colleague who is teaching similar courses to you, or call a team meeting if you are leading a particular subject or curriculum area. Informal meetings such as these probably don't have any rules, but some meetings in college are more formal, such as meetings of the college management or governors' meetings.

However, meetings are not universally welcomed by FE lecturers, especially when the workplace is not seen as supportive:

> I find that more and more meetings are, what can I say, non-optional, and I'm increasingly expected to attend at awkward times. There are aggressive emails sent about our obligations to do so. You're being made to feel guilty if you don't go – even if you're teaching. (Lecturer in creative arts)

The timing of meetings is difficult to arrange when lecturers have different timetables or are on a part-time contract. Another problem is the relevance of the meeting:

> I find meetings incredibly beneficial when they are about updating, about students, about curriculum. It is when they are about strategic planning, saving money, etc., as most of them are, that I feel I could be doing something else, not sitting there. I know that the head of department wants you to feel part and parcel of what is going on – but I can't make strategic decisions so do I need to be involved? I

can't change budgets, so it seems a waste of time. (Lecturer in beauty therapy)

If meetings were used less as occasions for informing lecturers of decisions made by college managers, and more as arenas for debate, then they would have more relevance to lecturers. When you are extremely busy and conscious of how much there is to be done in the time available, being drawn into wider college issues may not be a priority. Meetings are a way of trying to improve communications and involve lecturers in decision-making, and are an opportunity for you to learn about management practices and policies. If meetings are at the wrong time or don't seem relevant, then they become a source of frustration rather than an opportunity for learning how different parts of the college work and how they interact. It is difficult to focus on the 'big picture' if you feel stressed about planning your next lesson.

One answer might be to allocate a 'meetings time'. This has been tried in many colleges and is not always successful, but it conveys to lecturers that attendance at certain meetings is a part of your work commitment, and signals that your involvement is valued. Another strategy would be to make meetings shorter and more relevant, as these are two factors lecturers complain about the most as being lacking. Team briefings are a good example of short, relevant meetings. You might consider adopting them yourself for course team meetings and encouraging your head of department to adopt them for routine meetings.

Team briefings last about 10 to 30 minutes. If they are regular events, such as first thing every morning, 10 minutes would be enough time to let people know what is going on and why. If they are held less frequently, say once a week, then 30 minutes would be enough time for information-giving and an exchange of ideas. The idea behind team briefings is that they should be to the point and at a regular time that is convenient for the team.

USEFUL IDEAS

Team briefings

- Keep them short and stick to the time agreed.
- Have them regularly at a time when lecturers can attend.
- Meet in a convenient location.
- Inform lecturers of forthcoming events in the department and college.
- Provide information about *why* things are happening.
- Provide an opportunity for everyone to contribute.
- Provide an opportunity to ask questions or raise issues.
- Introduce new staff or staff changes.
- Create a positive communication channel.

Communicating with managers

The need for improved efficiency, and the introduction of more sophisticated IT systems, means that FE colleges are keen to adopt a 'flatter' hierarchy, and so the number of levels of management to be found in colleges is decreasing. This restructuring means managers assume responsibility for larger departments, schools or faculties, with overall responsibility for several curriculum areas that were previously managed separately. You could look on the positive side and acknowledge that restructuring provides the opportunity for developing management skills in the lecturer's role. Some lecturers do not look at things in this way and find changes resulting from restructuring difficult to accept. From their point of view, lecturers are constantly asked to implement new policies, which result in changed practices, without due preparation.

FE colleges have been delegated the responsibility through the LSC for the successful futures of millions of young people and adults, but concurrently have the responsibility to make the provision of education and training a successful business venture. Funding mechanisms and quality systems shape arrangements that purport to facilitate curriculum reform and development. In spite of that, it seems to many lecturers that it is the tasks concerned with accountability that occupy much of their time, rather than curriculum reform and development.

Two contrasting arguments are illustrated here. Martinez and Maynard (2002) suggest that there is evidence that lecturers do try to conform to management-led improvements, while grappling with their everyday world of teaching and learning. Their findings are that when management actions subsequently do not respect or support a lecturer's professional role, but instead focus on a lecturer's failure to achieve, the relationship between them deteriorates. The 'them–us' attitudes this encourages reflect a negative view of events according to Lumby and Tomlinson (2000:149), who challenge the idea that any group in the FE sector 'has a monopoly of professionalism, if such is taken to mean a primary commitment to students'. Their evidence shows that senior managers as well as lecturers may hold values that regard the interests of students as primary. If the disagreement is not on values, then it is on how these are best enacted.

Managing at a time of change needs to be more skilful than managing when there is stability, as accountability and control tend to take over and push out the creativity and innovation that is needed for future success (Ashcroft and James, 1998). Lumby and Tomlinson assert that senior managers are not so foolhardy as to imagine that they do not need to listen, communicate and build support. Most managers try to be as helpful and understanding as they can – particularly if you are new to a job. However, I am sure you have also experienced managers who are difficult to work with. Sometimes the workplace can almost seem like a battleground. Sometimes there are hidden agendas. You cannot always get everything right first time! When you are busy and under pressure, it is easy to forget to inform the office a student has left, mislay evaluation forms or not leave enough time to complete your annual course report. Your manager may also be under pressure to meet official deadlines and so their response may be sarcastic or patronizing, and they may say things such as 'Can't you even do a simple job like that?' or 'I don't know what you do with your time!'

If your manager says something disparaging about you or your work, it is not surprising that you get upset and even angry. You probably feel that you are on the receiving end of unfair criticism. Remember that you do not have to accept being spoken to in an inappropriate manner. Refer to the sarcastic or patronizing approach later when you are composed: that means separating the way the message was conveyed from the issue it was about. By approaching things in a constructive way you will leave yourself room to accept genuine reasons for your manager's comments.

It is not always easy to get the balance right between being willing and helpful and feeling that you are being put upon. Most lecturers are obliging, and managers are used to them 'helping out' all the time. Perhaps you have been a lecturer for a long time and have done more than your fair share of helping out, and decide enough is enough when more and more requests are made that eat into your preparation and marking time. Managers often ask you to do something *they* haven't got the time to do when they are overloaded themselves. They may ask you to stay after college, which means you miss out on something at home yet again. A manager's assertiveness may become bullying if they are not pleased with your response to the request. It is easy to say you have to stand up to bullying, but when you are demoralized it's very hard. Do you find it easy to say 'No' to your manager in these situations? Many lecturers do not. Sometimes you have to say 'No' to someone at work and really mean it. The following tips may prove useful if you don't find this easy to do.

USEFUL IDEAS

Saying 'no'

- Decide when it is justifiable to say 'No'.
- Apologize and give a good reason why you are declining the request.
- Mean what you say and repeat it if necessary.
- Suggest an alternative, e.g. 'I can't do that, but I can do . . . .'
- Be polite and firm and expect your decision to be respected.
- Saying 'No' does not mean that you alienate people and they will never approach you again to do special jobs.

If you look at the 'Useful Ideas' above, saying 'No' is something that needs to be thought through and considered. The following is a good example of how a lecturer said 'no' without feeling guilty or upsetting her manager.

LECTURER'S SURVIVAL STRATEGY

Do not assume others will be aggrieved by you saying 'No' – be assertive:

'I know that developing the Business Curriculum Centre is an important part of the department's plans and I appreciate you asking me to be involved. What you may not know is that I have agreed to take on the updating and renovation of the Training Office for administration students, so on this occasion I'll have to say no, as my priority must be to the project I'm already committed to. Thanks for thinking of me.' (Lecturer in business administration)

Often requests are made at the last minute, such as to stand in for your manager at a meeting or deal with a complaint from an irate employer. It may be that you are stopped in the corridor on your way to teach and asked if you would mind doing an urgent job. Don't agree to things just because you are rushed into them and then feel you cannot back out. Always ask for time to think before you make a decision, perhaps saying something like, 'I'm off to teach now. I'll think about it afterwards and see what I can do.'

It may be that you enjoy these additional responsibilities, and undertaking them is certainly a good way of broadening your experience. However, if you have already planned your work schedule for the week, think carefully about the extra work you will be taking on, or else you will end up going to class unprepared. Don't make snap decisions and regret them. If you take on a job, or do a favour, be clear why you said 'Yes'. If you accept the job it is up to you to take responsibility for it. After all, who is to say you're not going to learn something – especially self-management skills in doing your best in a difficult situation. With luck, your efforts will not go unnoticed.

Developing a wider role

As you become more familiar with your role as an FE lecturer, you may feel you want to widen your experience and start looking for positions that offer more responsibility and are more of a challenge. It may not necessarily be that you are frustrated in your present job. Looking for ways of developing your role can be prompted by positive experiences, for example spending time standing in for a colleague or leading a new curriculum initiative. Finding these experiences satisfying rather than stressful may cause you to question your current position and think about seeking a wider role. Realizing you are capable of shouldering responsibility may trigger thoughts about your future, but you have to be prepared to think beyond what affects you alone.

Reducing the number of layers of middle management has contributed to a general movement towards 'downsizing' in FE colleges, in an attempt to make savings on managerial and staffing costs. In turn, this has limited the opportunities for promotion for FE lecturers within colleges in the sector. If you are ambitious and want promotion, you have to be motivated. There are fewer rungs on the promotion ladder and so potentially more competition when you try to climb them. You may hear people say that luck plays a large part, for example being in the right place at the right time. I am sure you are aware of occasions when it is evident that promotions are made for reasons other than hard work or suitability. This notwithstanding, it is no coincidence that generally those who are promoted show the *potential* to grow into the new job. It is through demonstrating qualities in your current job that you communicate to others your ability and suitability for promotion. The *level* of your current work as a lecturer is not the critical factor – but the *standard* of it is crucial. What others discern in your current work is what you achieve. Your current achievements demonstrate your suitability for future promotion.

College managers have always delegated work but, because of restructuring, lecturers are now delegated areas of work that in the past would have been managed by a senior lecturer or head of department. The irony of flatter management structures in FE colleges is that lecturers undertake many tasks, but without the enhanced status or monetary rewards which would have been associated with them in the past. If you look at this in a positive way and recognize that preparing yourself for a future role is realized through doing your personal best in your current role, then it is important to identify the opportunities that these delegated tasks present. Thinking ahead in this way enables you to gain the experience now that will be useful in the future.

Don't expect anyone else to be as concerned about your future as you are. Remember that there are different strategies we can choose to select our routes towards preparing for promotion. What seems a good way forward for some lecturers may be inappropriate for others. You have to take the initiative and identify development opportunities, but not fall into the trap of assuming the college will necessarily support your choice or provide funding for it.

POTENTIAL PITFALLS

Stella is a conscientious and hard-working lecturer who thought her professional development relied simply on attendance at external courses, and so she undervalued the experience she was gaining doing a very responsible and worthwhile job. Read the following account of her experience and use the information to try to avoid the pitfalls Stella fell into in making the assumption that professional development is only achieved through attending courses:

All this information came through about staff development events and I'm ticking gaily through the list of appropriate ones. But when I present this to my manager the reply is you can't do this. It's not her fault, there's no money. But I think, 'I can't develop myself, I'm not getting the support I need.' (Lecturer in literacy and numeracy skills)

Attendance at staff development events is a good way of meeting others who share similar problems and is stimulating, but it is not the only way of developing yourself. Can you see beyond Stella's blinkered approach? Think about continuing to learn about the job of an FE lecturer as a dimension of practice, rather than just as the occasional updating at courses. This is how Oldroyd and Hall (1991:91) think about professional development when they say: 'It implies an improved capacity for control over one's working conditions.' Recognizing the learning opportunities gained through doing your day-to-day job is constructive, but it entails becoming better at controlling what you do from day to day.

It is certain that if you don't control your workplace experiences, others will. You will be reacting to decisions made by others rather than making your own decisions. What you need to survive is to develop the competence to direct your own learning.

CHECKOUT AND WORKOUT

Based on research with teachers of adults, Cranton (1996) identified that those engaged in their own professional development could be involved in the following activities:

- diagnosing development needs, with or without the assistance of others;
- setting development goals independently of pressure from others, but perhaps with the help of others;
- selecting sources of help for learning: materials, individuals, consultants, courses or programs;
- determining what is personally meaningful, apart from the reward systems of the institution or organization;
- choosing to give up independent learning temporarily in order to gain knowledge and skills in a more formal setting;
- continuously reviewing the progress made in the chosen professional development activities;
- honestly acknowledging weaknesses and shortcomings;
- changing tactics when the current strategy is not meeting needs;
- evaluating professional development progress based on personal criteria.

Are you engaged in any of these activities? It is difficult to make decisions if your workplace experiences are negative or life appears to be out of control when you are stressed or overloaded. Remember that the above is a list of activities that teachers of adults *actually used* to manage their learning.

Work out which activities you need to employ to manage your own learning. Think of the list as presenting possible self-management goals and consider how you could apply them to your situation.

If you hope to grow and develop through your practice, you have to look beyond the classroom or workshop. How you do this is not clear cut. There are no rules for guaranteeing success in the future, and you will have to make judgements according to your particular situation in college and the changing circumstances in the Learning and Skills sector. You will need to develop an awareness of what your future role might involve. If you do get promotion what are the requirements and expectations? You may need to think about:

- obtaining formal qualifications, such as a higher degree or advanced vocational qualification;
- developing competence in particular administrative/ managerial tasks;
- working on your leadership skills.

As a lecturer you have to *interpret* what will be expected – sometimes you get it right and sometimes you get it wrong. Developing your professional judgement in this way and interpreting future workplace requirements more accurately is the key to thriving rather than just surviving in an FE college.

Appraisal provides an opportunity to judge various aspects of your work by looking back at how you have performed in the past and then by looking forward to agree future targets. Your appraisal is an opportunity to discuss your workplace experience, so it is important to be clear about its purpose. One of the functions of appraisal is for you and your appraiser to assess your potential and predict the level and type of work you are capable of doing in the future. Another function of appraisal is to help you plan how to reach your full potential so that the college can benefit fully from your talents and abilities. However, you need to be aware of the conflicting roles your appraiser has to perform: that of judge and mentor. Additionally, the appraiser is concerned with organizational goals; you are more likely to be concerned with personal goals, and these may not coincide. Appraisals are often presented as a way of reviewing your work objectively, but in practice dispositions that reveal a potential for promotion, such as enthusiasm, application and resourcefulness, are judged subjectively. As long as you do not relinquish control of your own professional development, appraisal can be an important time for reflecting about what accomplishments need to be in place that are not now. The following ideas will help you focus on the process.

USEFUL IDEAS

Appraisal

- Prepare well – completing any forms required is a good way of self-appraising before the interview.
- Don't focus on past achievements too much – leave time to think about the future.
- Recognize that there may be a conflict of roles.
- Plan your goals for the coming year, getting your appraiser to agree them.
- Ask how your plans could fit into the college plans – but put your own point of view.
- Ask for feedback – listen to what your appraiser has to say.
- Use appraisal as an opportunity to solve current workplace problems.
- Discuss support or funding for formal qualifications.
- Ask for your appraiser's opinion about your future potential – but remember that is all it is: their opinion.

If your appraisal has gone well, then you can thank the appraiser for their help and advice. You now know what you are aiming for. It is up to you to prove you can achieve it. If your appraisal has gone badly, you should go to the Human Resource department for help, as you can ask for an appraisal to be done by someone else. An alternative to conventional appraisal schemes is peer appraisal, which provides accountability to your peer group.

In this chapter, the intention was to help you think about how you respond to workplace experience and to use it constructively. The following quote in Food for Thought may help you to reflect on your own readiness to learn.

FOOD FOR THOUGHT

Your first introduction to ideas about learning may have been encountered when you did your initial teaching qualification. Minton's (2005) advice holds good today for every FE lecturer, however much experience you may have gained since you qualified:

> We talk about growing with the job. Learning is growth through experience. We need to grow as teachers and stimulate growth in our students. There is no short cut. Some grow and flourish more quickly than others do. This is not simply a matter of luck. It is more a readiness to learn – to reflect on experience and to explore alternative methods and approaches. It may depend on ability to adapt and willingness to take risks, to engage in creative problem-solving. It depends crucially on our belief in ourselves. (Minton, 2005:6)

Using workplace experience constructively means exploring alternatives and being more creative in the way you solve workplace problems. To achieve this, you have to develop confidence in yourself. There may be an element of luck and 'being in the right place at the right time' but as Minton says, it is 'not simply a matter of luck'. If you are ready to learn, you will be able to climb the promotion ladder as and when opportunities arise, and so put all your hard work to good use.

---

4 Developing positive relationships

In Chapter 2, it was argued that being effective as an FE lecturer was primarily about how you deal with people rather than tasks; and it was suggested in Chapter 3 that getting the best out of workplace experience depends on you developing confidence in yourself. These two notions are linked in this chapter. The emphasis is on the need to develop an awareness of the ways you can build professional relationships with colleagues, students, employers and other stakeholders in order to cope with the demands and expectations of your work as an FE lecturer.

Your professional relationship with colleagues and students can make or break your success in your job. An FE lecturer works with all kinds of people. You may not like all of them, and indeed they may not all like you! Other people can be a prime source of stress, particularly colleagues who get on your nerves or students who wind you up and drive you mad. Have you ever thought about whether you might play a part in creating these reactions in others? After all, a relationship is two-sided. Poor relationships with colleagues or students affect your enjoyment of your job. Many of you will have experienced the feeling of dejection over a disagreement with a colleague or a confrontation with a student.

You cannot hope to like everyone you work with and meet in college but, if you want to succeed, you have to develop survival strategies to cope with their foibles and shortcomings – and develop an awareness of your own! Nearly everyone has some weaknesses in the way they relate to others. As an FE lecturer, you will have to work at developing positive relationships with colleagues, students and employers if you want to survive. Becoming a lecturer is not just a matter of acquiring a qualification to do a job, nor even about acquiring the skills and competences to develop your confidence to do a good job. It is also about respecting the people around you in college and in the community and developing positive relationships with them.

Working well with colleagues

An ability to work effectively with colleagues is essential, as more and more the picture of the FE lecturer isolated in the classroom and working single-handedly outside it is becoming a thing of the past. Working with others, whether developing a curriculum, devising resources or delivering and assessing students' work, is probably a more realistic picture of the way many FE lecturers work today. You may be in a team of lecturers who work in the same department, teach the same subject, deliver different modules on the same course or perform the same function across the college, for example internal verification or peer assessment. Colleagues work together to make maximum use of each other's experience and ability in order to reach the group's goals. However capable or talented individual lecturers may be, if they are unable to communicate with each other, say because of personality clashes and conflicts, then it is difficult to achieve what they set out to do.

Communicating with colleagues and getting on with them is becoming more important, as working collaboratively is now an expectation of the role and college structures presume this. A very experienced lecturer outlines the reality of working well with others.

LECTURER'S SURVIVAL STRATEGY

Work together with colleagues, not in competition with them:

When you work in a team there are advantages but there are things you have to let go in order to work effectively. One of these is, to a certain extent, competitiveness and a feeling that you're going to use the product of whatever you're doing to further your career. I find the benefits of working in a team − or trying to work in a team — are greater than being competitive. The reason is survival. People begin to realize that they need one another. We deal with some challenging groups and it is very important for us to talk a lot about what we're doing. (Lecturer in foundation studies)

It can be seen from this lecturer's experience that working well with colleagues is not always easy. However, the account makes it clear that you can survive if you work together and support each other. This presupposes you all work well together and complement each other. However hard-working or keen you are, if the group doesn't function as a whole, your efforts may be wasted. Often, personal differences mean that lecturers work at cross purposes and go off in different directions and 'do their own thing'. A good starting point if you want to raise your self-awareness is to focus on how *you* work with others and come across to others.

FOOD FOR THOUGHT

Your effectiveness in working with others depends very much on your individual communication skills and the way you deploy them in particular situations.

- Identify the strengths you bring to working with others. Think of occasions when your positive relationships with others helped in completing a task successfully.
- Identify the weaknesses you exhibit in working with others. Think of examples when you clashed with colleagues.

A realistic assessment of your strengths and weaknesses will enable you to develop an awareness of the type of behaviour you adopt in different situations.

Working with colleagues does not mean that you either have to agree with everything they say, or argue until you get your own point of view across. What it does mean is exploring issues with them or resolving a problem in a way that satisfies everyone. To do this, you have to contribute to the discussions effectively. If you promise to do something just to please others, then don't do it because you took on too much, relationships break down. When you are reticent and avoid a discussion or put off contributing your views until another time, you lose the opportunity to practise and improve your communication skills. Your colleagues cannot read your mind: to survive you have to develop the capacity to share your thoughts and feelings professionally on work issues.

For some lecturers, expressing their opinion in a professional manner comes naturally. However, others avoid threatening situations. A complete breakdown in relationships is apparent in the following account of a lecturer's experience of negative criticism from a colleague over a long period.

POTENTIAL PITFALLS

Jon experienced adverse criticism for three years, which undermined him. Eventually things got to a point where Jon did something about it.

Towards the end of last summer term the atmosphere in our office was absolutely horrendous. I moved out of one office to another because I was feeling physically ill being with a certain member of staff who made my life hell for three years: constantly criticizing and not really being aware of what he was doing, always undermining me, and saying I was never doing things properly. It was constant: on a day-to-day basis. Since I've moved out I have found that he does it to others. But I nearly broke down over it. I nearly resigned over it. (Lecturer in IT)

Jon's experience is appalling and allowing the criticism to go on for so long had a devastating effect. What Jon failed to do was tackle the issue. This is understandable, as when you are constantly being undermined you feel threatened and your confidence dips. There is nothing worse than feeling that a key area of your working life, such as your day-to-day interaction with a member of your department, isn't going well. However, when you are in this situation, trying to change it appears too difficult to contemplate. Even small things seem too big to tackle. The trouble is that if you don't deal with them, and if you don't make choices or changes – choices will be made for you. The best plan is to take the plunge and do something rather than feeling overwhelmed and putting off decisions. Avoiding the situation can take more energy and cause you more grief in the long run.

Most of us aren't very good at receiving criticism and react badly, but it is important to deal with it, otherwise you end up believing what your colleague says and may risk becoming incapable of doing anything, as your confidence drains away.

CHECKOUT AND WORKOUT

It is important to handle criticism well. If you experience negative criticism about your work, check out how you handle it.

1   Do you usually try to brush off what is being said?
2   Do you often jump to the wrong conclusions?
3   Do you always feel the criticism is not deserved?
4   Do you find it difficult to express your own opinion when challenged?
5   Do you find it difficult to remain calm when being criticized?
6   Do you usually refuse to apologise?

If you answered 'Yes' to any of the questions, you are probably focusing on the way the criticism was made rather than on what it was about. Adverse criticism delivered insensitively can be hard to take and the results can shatter your self-confidence.

Remember, it is important to receive criticism professionally in order to avoid a breakdown in communication between you and your colleagues. Use the following pointers as a self-check for handling criticism and work out a strategy for the future:

- Try to listen carefully.
- Respond only to the facts – not the way the criticism was delivered.

- Be fair – the criticism may be justified.
- Recognize why your actions attract criticism.
- Try to remain calm – don't say too much if you're angry.
- Ask for advice on how to avoid the situation in future.
- Ignore personal comments – deal with them later after a 'cooling-off' period.
- Don't shout or argue in the staff room – or burst into tears.
- If you are really angry or upset, find somewhere to be on your own and gain your composure.
- Try to put the criticism behind you. Learn from the experience and don't hold a grudge.

To avoid potential pitfalls (such as the ones Jon fell into), act on the advice and acknowledge the reasons that put you in a vulnerable position in the first place. Take steps to avoid exposing yourself to the same criticism again by talking to supportive colleagues if there is a problem. Remember what it feels like to be criticized as, whatever your role in college, there will be occasions when you have to speak to others about things that have gone wrong or that you are not happy with. There are however ways of criticizing a colleague constructively, as the following 'Useful Ideas' illustrate. Use the scenario between a course tutor and a course team member to help you devise a conversation for an issue you need to tackle.

USEFUL IDEAS

Giving criticism

1　Choose a suitable time and a location where you can have a conversation in private. Don't allow too much time between the invitation and the appointment time.
2　Broach the specific issue straightaway.
3　Invite a response to the criticism.
4　Summarize the response and try to get an agreement.
5　Get suggestions about changes you want to happen.
6　Discuss and summarize the ideas and agree on a solution.

---

7 Thank them for coming and close the meeting promptly.

Suggestions

1 *I'd like to talk to you about the student evaluations for the module you've just completed. Would 11 o'clock in the interview room by reception be OK?*
2 *The students' evaluations reveal that you're always late for your Thursday evening class.*
3 *Is this what is happening?*
4 *It's clear you have a problem on Thursdays that causes you to be late.*
5 *How can you go about getting to that class on time? What can you do?*
6 *So let's agree that in future to avoid poor evaluations you . . .*
7 *Thanks for giving your time to sort this out.*

Use the above 'Useful Ideas' to give you some thoughts about how to approach tricky situations and avoid undermining relationships with colleagues. Plan what you want to say beforehand step-by-step. It is still not easy to carry out, as your colleague may challenge the criticism, feel threatened by it or get upset if there is a genuine problem. If the criticism is justified, then be assertive when you address the issues, but don't be judgemental. Don't tell your colleague what to do – ask them what *they* plan to do. Put yourself in their shoes and you will be more likely to handle such situations effectively. Be aware of the other person and give a thought to their needs and feelings. You can't enforce their cooperation, but you can acknowledge that someone has a problem and be ready to discuss ideas about how they can resolve it. In this way, you can keep the communication channels open and demonstrate concern for your colleague, as well as for sorting out the problem.

Many FE lecturers mistakenly feel that to survive you need to protect yourself from embarrassment and conflict. In a team meeting or a staff room discussion, you may have observed how someone intervened and stopped others discussing opposing views, or let someone take over and change the subject to avoid a difference of opinion. A better strategy would be to face up to the disagreements rather than smooth them over. It may be that the atmosphere is tense for a while, but in the long run everyone knows where they stand.

Forging links with employers

I asked a particularly successful lecturer if they could identify anything that they did in the course of their work that had contributed to their development as a lecturer. The answer was interesting and not one I anticipated:

> *Two things come to mind immediately. Passing of information between colleagues – often informally over coffee. The other is visiting students on work placement, seeing them working with children, talking to supervisors and looking at displays of children's work with teachers.* (Lecturer in early years education)

What this lecturer clearly describes is the benefit of networking. Networking involves interacting with others in an informal way: both with colleagues, and individuals outside college. Settings for such meetings are often in corridors, common rooms and, as in the case above, eating areas. Time spent with colleagues in informal discussion is an excellent way of exchanging ideas and information and developing new insights about workplace issues. Such discussions are purposeful, but often include non-work-related issues. The significance of networking is building up positive social relationships with people that may benefit both of you professionally.

Informal networks extend beyond college too. As in the example above, meeting a student's workplace supervisor is an opportunity not only to chat about the student's progress, but also to question them about current workplace issues and provide information about how the student is doing in college, or inform them of impending changes involving the vocational qualification. Spending time in conversation with others in this way establishes contacts that are mutually beneficial. Observing what is going on in the workplace and talking to colleagues on your return to college also keeps everyone up to date with what is going on, and engages them in learning about their vocational area in an informal way.

Working in partnership with others, and cooperating with them for the benefit of the students, rather then being in competition with them, are successful survival strategies, as the following cases clearly show.

LECTURERS' SURVIVAL STRATEGIES

Support workplace assessors:

I share my resources with assessors in the workplace. The assessors and I meet regularly every month at least and if they need questions to give to clients they'll come to me and I'm quite happy to share with them as they keep me informed about what's going on in the industry. I say to them, 'If you have any difficulties just contact me and I will give you some examples that I've assessed.' (Lecturer in construction)

Work together with employers for the benefit of trainees:

The priorities of the employer are to cover shifts. They have minimum staffing allocations and can't spare people from their workforce every Thursday to come to college. I've spoken to lots of employers about this and I've come up with a course delivered once a month on the employer's premises. On that day we'll do underpinning knowledge and some direct observation assessments. The employer's happy with that and we keep our numbers up. (Lecturer in care)

Keep employers informed about students they sponsor:

As course leader on the National Certificate, I deal with employers of day release students. We've started doing interim reports for them at the end of each term. We've had a lot of positive feedback about this and it's helped because the students are aware that their employers are going to have a much better idea of how they're doing in college and consequently they're performing slightly better. I think it'll help retention and achievement. I mean, that's the other reason for doing it, it's not just for the employers' sake; it's to help us as well. (Lecturer in mechanical engineering)

Building positive relationships with others outside college clearly has benefits for the colleague as well as employers. Other ideas used by lecturers include:

- informing employers of examination results speedily;
- invitations to exhibitions, Open Days, prize-giving and graduation ceremonies;
- sending a newsletter with information about a course or student;
- writing to thank employers for their cooperation in supplying visiting speakers or organizing visits.

Respecting students

Creating positive relationships with students is sometimes problematic for FE lecturers. You have to learn how to be friendly and approachable without being overfamiliar. Getting this balance right is the key to building relationships with students, but is not an easy one to achieve: it has to be worked at. If you are too formal or authoritarian, you take the risk of alienating students. They might find the atmosphere repressive or even threatening. The answer is not necessarily to be too laid back either. It is up to the lecturer to demonstrate through their behaviour what is expected in their sessions and to articulate guidelines as to why. It is important that these are expressed in positive rather than negative terms. If you don't make clear your expectations and look carefully at your own reactions when problems arise, you may end up shouting and throwing your weight around when faced with a noisy or uncooperative group. This stresses you out and is certainly not conducive to creating a learning environment. It is easy to fall into the trap of being negative. The following viewpoint, volunteered by a colleague, about the qualities required for developing relationships with students, demonstrates this:

I think you need to be as tough as old boots. I think that's a major attribute. Students seem out to get you. They trip you up. They are constantly critical of things you do. I've found you have to develop a thick skin and learn to dodge the big punches. They're going to whinge about something whether it's justified or not. Tell us we've been teaching them bunkum. You need to be caring, but with a suit of armour. (Lecturer in Business Studies)

This viewpoint reveals that for the above lecturer, working with students is often an exasperating experience. Students identify with a lecturer's mood and respond accordingly. If the lecturer's expectation is that students are always ready to whinge about something, then it is likely that this will be the behaviour that he notices. Positive relationships are difficult to build in such a situation.

In any group, both the lecturer and students play a part in the way the group functions. There needs to be recognition that each student brings their own experiences and expectations to a group – as does the lecturer. However, it is your style as a lecturer and your personal characteristics that are a major factor in creating the atmosphere within the group. In the above example, is there a gap between what the students are looking for and what this lecturer is providing in his sessions? Is the students' tendency to want to trip up the lecturer a reaction to his own critical fault-finding?

The way to survive in this situation is not to focus on your concerns, for example the negative feelings you have because students are constantly critical of things you do. Focus on the students' concerns, that is, why they are critical. What is causing them to be like that?

Students are not always equipped to air their grievances considerately. They may find differences between what you are telling them in class and their own experiences at work and just come out with 'That's rubbish! That's not how we do it.' Students don't need constant condemnation for the way they express themselves. They may be right and you may be out of touch – on other occasions, it could be the other way around. Despite this, they need opportunities as students to learn how to express themselves more considerately through reasonable dialogue with the lecturer about such matters. Building up acceptable working relationships with students is a gradual process. If learners cannot stand out as good students and earn respect for their college work, they may do outrageous things to gain attention and significance. Creating an environment where learning flourishes rarely happens spontaneously. You may well have your work cut out if you want to survive and teach students to seek significance in more socially acceptable ways.

Rather than being 'as tough as old boots' as the lecturer in Business Studies advocates, the primary attribute for a lecturer above all according to Rogers (2002) is tact, that is knowing what is fitting to do or say in dealing with people or circumstances. In the example below, another colleague did not mention tact when asked the same question about the qualities that are important in developing relationships with students. This may be because developing and using professional knowledge is a largely tacit and intuitive process, and linking professional values, and practical experience often occurs below the level of conscious self-reflection according to Elliott, (1991). However, she displayed an intuitive perception of tact:

> *I think you need to be somebody who actually likes adolescents, who can cope with toddler tantrums! You need to have a sense of humour and be prepared to put in a lot of effort to build a relationship. The majority of students in our department are 16 to 19 and have very strong ideas about what they think is right in the world and usually see all adults as being a threat or not being people they can actually talk to. I think you need to be able to overcome those things.*
> (GNVQ Co-ordinator)

Much of the best practice in college is based on the kind of intuitive judgement that the GNVQ coordinator displays. It is often only when lecturers experience dilemmas that they are prompted into self-reflection.

Your students may not be adolescents like those described above, but may appear to act like them. Hanson's (1996:103) research with full-time mature students found that 'adults [are] prepared to suspend their adulthood at the door of the institution'. Adults returning to learning are faced with many new situations – both positive and negative. When students have 'toddler tantrums' and start to lose their temper, or are sarcastic or sulky, they are acting as spoiled children. Hanson contends that this does not make them children again, but says that students are willing to accept what is in effect an unequal relationship in college (between adult-as-student and adult-as-lecturer), as long as the lecturer has something to offer. Once this is not the case, they no longer either willingly accept the learning tasks lecturers set them or adapt to the methods used, and the positive relationship is broken. What this means is that respect as a lecturer has to be *earned* from your students, it cannot be assumed.

Respect can be gained by keeping the atmosphere light but firm but, more importantly, it can be gained by the way you manage your teaching to support students' learning. Ideas about this are included in Chapter 5. Your efforts in building relationships should not be about winning popularity with students, but about treating them respectfully and fairly. Students find it difficult to respect a lecturer if they feel they are being treated unfairly. If you are brusque, unreasonably demanding and belittle students, there is a strong possibility that it will create resentment. The argument that 'students asked for it' is not an acceptable excuse for their unfair treatment. You must look at your own efforts to build positive relationships. Obviously, when students do outrageous things to seek attention or feel significant, it is more difficult to relate positively to them. Nevertheless, if you expect to be treated with consideration, you have to treat students with consideration first. What that entails may vary from group to group, as the same factors are not appropriate for a group of young students on day release from school for vocational training as they are for a group of full-time students of various ages on a higher education course. Research shows that what works, or is deemed good practice in one learning site, may not work or be good practice in another (Hodkinson and James, 2003). Students from different cultures may have different ideas about conveying respect. A charming example of this that I encountered is of a lecturer, Mrs Watson, who said to her students — a group of mainly female, newly arrived international students — 'call me Dawn'. They duly called her 'Mrs Dawn'. The lecturer's invitation to be less formal in the classroom was not one the group responded to.

Relationships with students are influenced by a complex combination of individual, social and cultural factors. You cannot change students overnight, so don't focus on instant remedies. Make it your aim to allow students time to assimilate what it means to participate in learning in your sessions. There is no standardized approach to building positive relationships. However, they all depend on good communication – that is, talking and listening. The value of good communication cannot be overemphasized. Curzon (2003:126) describes the primary function of communication in the teaching process brilliantly as 'the creation of a commonality of thought and feeling which leads to learning'. Positive relationships with students help create learning opportunities for them as Curzon described, as they are able to express their thoughts and articulate their feelings without fear of rejection or ridicule. Frequent conversations facilitate learning and have the power to transform students' perspectives as well as the relationship between you and the students.

CHECK OUT AND WORKOUT

Communicating with students

How well do you talk to your students?

Small courtesies such as the following make college life more pleasant:

- Greet them at the start of the session in a welcoming manner.
- Say please and thank you when collecting in work or handing it back.
- Call students by their names – and get those names right.
- Sound calm, not cross, by keeping your temper under control and not shouting.
- Respond to their questions and show you value their opinion by your positive language.
- Avoid cutting them off in mid-sentence.
- Only make promises you can keep – don't agree to things to keep the peace.

The language you use is important, as is your tone of voice. If you demonstrate the type of relationship you want with students, it may not happen overnight, but at least there is a chance that it might eventually.

How well do you listen to your students?

Listening carefully to students in the following ways shows you appreciate them and their views:

- Concentrate and show you are listening by nodding and smiling and looking at them.
- Avoid staring at students, so they don't feel threatened.
- Avoid letting your eyes wander round the room while someone is talking to you.
- Listen without saying, 'Go on, I'm listening' while hunting around for the handouts to distribute.
- Listen without interrupting and be prepared to let others have their say.
- Listen without assuming you know what someone is going to say and so stopping paying attention.
- Listen without thinking about what you want to say in reply: concentrate instead on what is being said.
- Listen and then slow down and pause before you answer – you stand a better chance of listening effectively.

The effectiveness of any communication will obviously be influenced by how articulate the students are. You have to be prepared to interpret what is said and spend time helping students to express their thoughts clearly and logically. Often you have to think about what is really behind the words actually being used. When you are interpreting the message that students are conveying to you, you depend a lot on the tone of voice they use and the body language they exhibit. One of the interesting yet disquieting things about body language is that a student might be sending out all sorts of messages they do not want to convey. Posture and facial expression may be at odds with the words they are saying:

- If a student is slouched over the desk or laid back in the chair – are they bored or just relaxed?

- If a student is hunched up and tense – are they nervous or just cold or tired?
- If a student is alert and leaning forward – are they showing aggression or interest?
- If a student is sitting with arms folded, pursed lips and legs crossed – are they unsure about what you mean or being uncooperative?

Look for more than one instance of body language – don't rely on one signal as this is often misleading. Unless you observe students carefully, you will not pick up these signals and will not understand why they are unable to do what you asked or to join in the session.

Not all students are committed to their college courses and, however hard you try, some students may remain negative and uncooperative. Sometimes there are deep issues and funda-mental differences to be dealt with. Nevertheless, it is your responsibility to initiate and work out an agreement about a way of working that does not hinder learning for others. This may not always work out successfully. A few ideas for dealing with classroom challenges are given in Chapter 5.

If you want to build positive relationships with students, you can usually do so during your teaching sessions. However, you are often faced with the challenges of communicating with diverse individuals in a large group. Developing your awareness of how you talk to and listen to students and how you recognize their body language is best done when you are dealing with students one to one – for instance in tutorials.

USEFUL IDEAS

Tutorials: how to gain respect

- Be clear and precise about what the tutorial is for, e.g. to check progress, about missing a hand-in date or frequent absence, preparation for assignment.
- Set out the student's objectives. If the student is reluctant to talk, set out your objectives. It might be difficult to get students to say things face to face that they say behind your back.
- Deal with issues from the student's perspective first if you can, then construct a *shared* view of what this raises and consider various sides of the problem. Explain that both of you win if you go for what both of you want.
- Get the student to start thinking about what you can get agreement on. Ask the student 'What can *you* do now?'
- Promote harmony rather than conflict and don't get into an argument. Say: 'It's not working – so what now?'
- If necessary, present a compromise. Show the student you genuinely want a resolution.
- Be seen to be fair and honest – fairness is usually valued above everything by students.
- Remember non-verbal messages are revealing.

Often you have to complete a tutorial record form, and this is a useful tool for summarizing what has gone on. Try to agree on:

1 What is to be done and when.
2 How it is to be done.
3 Who is available to provide support, e.g. IT, student services, learning resources.
4 What will happen if the agreement is not kept.
5 Tutorial time to discuss progress.

Remember, an agreement means very little without a relationship, so the tutorial is a time to invest in the relationship that makes the agreement possible. Relationship building is an important outcome – so don't make your investment about getting your own way at all costs. A clear, mutually understood agreement up-front is a measure of your success and this creates guidelines against which the student can measure his or her own success in the weeks to come.

FOOD FOR THOUGHT

Excellence in teaching and learning depends on how well a lecturer and students work together. It is not about friendship, but it is about setting the tone for building positive relationships. Carl Rogers (1983) provides some advice on how this can be achieved when he says, 'that which is most personal is most general'. What he is saying is that the more authentic you become and the more genuine when talking and listening to others – particularly regarding personal experiences and self-doubts – the more others can relate to you and the safer it makes them feel to express themselves.

---

5 Creating a learning environment

A popular image of an FE lecturer's work is one of preparing lessons, teaching students and marking. These activities are seen as the essence of a lecturer's work, and remain central to their perception of what the job entails, despite the considerable changes within the sector described by Ellington (2000:311):

> The role of the university and college lecturer is changing. Traditionally, their main role was to teach, i.e. to impart knowledge to their students via lectures and similar face-to-face activities. Now, it is becoming increasingly widely recognised that their main role is to help their students to learn, something that requires a fairly radical change in how they work.

A reappraisal of the lecturer's role, such as Ellington describes, affects the relationship between lecturer and student and changes the activities in which each is involved in the classroom or workshop. Attempts to modernize teaching and learning transform the social relations in college and play down activities that previously were regarded as central to a lecturer's identity and sense of worth (Avis, 1999). In recent years, there has been a shift away from lecturing and formal whole-group instruction. What is currently considered good practice is student-centred learning, whether it is class based, e-learning or blended learning. However, good practice is always a matter under discussion in a climate of change, and opinions about what is good teaching and learning vary. Supporting, facilitating and enabling learning are now pivotal. Nowadays, imparting knowledge of their subject specialism – which in the past has been at the core of a lecturer's professional identity – is no longer their main role, as the nature of teaching is changing. If you are newly qualified and have recently joined the FE sector, you will be familiar with the notion of the modern lecturer as a person who assists students to learn for themselves (Reece and Walker, 2003). Focusing on learning is not new, but learning has been brought into prominence over recent years through various government policies promoting learning – all under the banner of lifelong learning (DfEE, 1998; DfEE, 1999; DfES, 2002).

For some lecturers who have been working in the FE sector for a while, this presents a dilemma. There is a gap between their perceptions of the role as a subject teacher and the perceptions of policy-makers and college managers that lecturers should be developing strategies which focus on the promotion of students' learning. There is a fear among many lecturers that if they develop resources for student-directed learning, or encourage e-learning, they will be doing themselves out of their own job. For these lecturers, it is often this fear, and the realization that their traditional role is becoming redundant, that has proved stressful.

It may well be that at the root of this dilemma is the long-held practice of appointing lecturers for their professional or vocational qualifications and business or industrial experiences, rather than their qualifications in teaching (or even appointing lecturers without a teaching qualification – but with a commitment to obtain one). In my experience, FE lecturers seem to struggle with the notion of their professional identity as they come into the sector through very different routes and tend to identify with their discipline or industrial background rather than teaching as their profession. This identity crisis is compounded when learning takes priority over teaching.

Giving some thought to the concept of the lecturer's role confirms the importance of a theme that has been running through this *Survival Guide*: the diversity of the FE sector. This implies that what is an appropriate learning environment in one situation may not be appropriate or work in another. If you are a lecturer in psychology, creating a learning environment for supervising a dissertation for a final-year student on a degree course is very different from the way a lecturer in catering and hospitality working with NVQ1 Food Preparation and Food Service students needs to do it. Quite simply, not only does an academic/vocational divide exist but also there will be differences in the actual physical environment – a library study centre or training kitchen and restaurant – and the timescale and complexity of the learning activities. The situation in which teaching and learning takes place is a key determinant of how the learning environment takes shape (Armitage *et al.*, 2003). Each situation is unique, so calls for creativity on the part of lecturers.

When you are considering ways of creating a learning environment, you have to recognize that much depends on a whole array of factors such as your subject, the age and ability of the students, the size of the group and the resources available. Nevertheless, there are important elements in the way successful lecturers work that seem to be effective in creating a learning environment and are worthy of consideration. There are certain coping strategies that successful lecturers use when faced with change that may provide practical ideas for you to think about. The way in which these lecturers work contributes to a positive learning environment, particularly the way they:

- plan their teaching and learning strategies;
- structure the day-to-day organization of their sessions;
- deal with classroom challenges.

These three interrelated themes are examined in this chapter.

In this chapter you are also invited to examine your own ways of working, your own concept of the lecturer's role and your response to the focus in the FE sector on learner control. It is critical to remember that your activities are the only things under your *direct* control. Learning is not a product of teacher activity. However, your activities form the lever you can use to bring about desirable conditions for your students' learning. What you do to instigate or sustain certain activities with students in your sessions, and how your students respond to these, will enable you to identify ways of supporting students. In turn, this will enable them gradually to take control of their own learning more effectively. Rather than resisting pedagogical change, this knowledge will allow you to think more clearly about your own pedagogical approach and develop successful survival strategies to cope with pedagogical change.

Planning teaching and learning

For the majority of you, what you are expected to teach – that is, the subject content – is prescribed and set out in a syllabus, specification, prospectus or module definition of some kind. These documents contain indicative content, course objectives, learning outcomes or performance criteria. The syllabus is devised by an examination board, professional body or vocational consortium. How you put the syllabus into practice, however, is your task. You have to transform the information from the syllabus into a course schedule, programme of study, scheme of work or learning programme. When you develop a learning programme from a syllabus you have to take into account:

> ... teaching a range of different group sizes, the selection and use of a variety of teaching methods, the creation of teaching aids, resources and displays, the design of assessment tasks including examinations and, in particular, the concatenation of these into a year-long course. The last requires the highest level of problem-solving skills if it is to be done well. (Clow, 2005:79)

Clow brings together the numerous elements you need to take into account when planning teaching and learning. As Clow points out, it is the concatenation, the linking together, of these numerous elements that is challenging if it is to be done well. A highly motivated and well-qualified lecturer confessed to me after her first year as a full-time lecturer that she found the process of producing new learning programmes 'overwhelming'. Developing a new course or revising one that has been running for some time are tasks that require the highest level of problem-solving skills and are challenging for even the most experienced lecturers.

If you look at the syllabus for your course, is it clear and coherent? This is the intention of the syllabus: to help lecturers plan teaching and learning. However, it does not put content in order of importance, or identify what is essential to know, say how long each component might take. The syllabus does not indicate how you put it into practice. It is this ambiguity that makes developing learning programmes challenging. The importance of developing a viable programme can be seen in the following case study.

POTENTIAL PITFALLS

A part-time lecturer, Theresa, who was a new member of a course team, became stressed because she was presented with a course programme that did not reflect the current syllabus.

I took up an appointment as a part-time lecturer to teach on a training course for further and adult education lecturers. As I had recently taught this course in another college, I was pretty confident about what I'd taken on. What I didn't anticipate was that radical changes introduced two years before had just been 'bolted on' to the old scheme of work by my new colleagues. The course team were familiar with the content of the old course, knew what to look for in assessments and were reluctant, as they put it, to 'ditch what worked'. The result was that not only had the students to complete assignments relating to the old scheme, but they had also to complete additional ones to meet the new requirements. So, they were overloaded and confused and deadlines were difficult to meet. For lecturers, there was increased marking so everyone ended up stressed out – even the external examiner! (Lecturer in education studies)

The case study shows that learning about how to organize teaching and learning requires a departmental context which is supportive: and this may be difficult to achieve in some circumstances. Course content often changes as it is brought in line with new policies and practices, or updated to meet new vocational regulations. The stress that Theresa described in the above case study was experienced because the course team failed to *link together* the new course requirements with redesigned assessments. It is tempting to incorporate new requirements into the old framework to save time and effort. But, as can been seen from Theresa's experience, this creates problems rather than solves them. You don't have to ditch what works –

but good practice means you have to revise the learning programme thoroughly and update it to meet current course requirements. Successful ideas can be integrated into the new assessments. After all, the changes should create an environment that improves conditions for student learning – it is not meant to stress everyone out!

Revising a learning programme provides an opportunity to collaborate with colleagues and not only share the work but also share conversations about important questions such as: why were the changes introduced? What new ideas or policies underpin the changes? Are the changes fundamental or minor? Such conversations can prove rewarding and motivating and provide an opportunity for you to use and develop your professional judgement and problem-solving skills to make decisions about the required changes.

Additionally, it is during such conversations that you often become aware of your own attitudes to teaching and learning and engage in lively discussions with colleagues about the way the learning programme should be designed. The reason for this is that we all bring our own values and assumptions about teaching and learning to the role of FE lecturer. Planning changes in practice is often a trigger for making your own values explicit. It is often through discussion with colleagues who hold differing views that you are able to clarify your own thinking and reach new insights. The process of becoming aware of your attitudes to teaching and learning is important because the ambiguity in a syllabus provides a degree of latitude in implementation and allows for interpretation. The 'Check-out and Workout' is designed to encourage you to reflect on the values you bring to planning teaching and learning and interpreting the syllabus.

CHECKOUT AND WORKOUT

Use the following questions and examples to help you reflect on your educational values and make them explicit:

- What is the importance of further education for your students?
- What aspects of your role as an FE lecturer are important for your professional identity?
- What aspects of good practice do you consider should be incorporated into planning teaching and learning?
- What inspires you and gives you satisfaction when teaching?

A negative staff room culture is unlikely to generate discussion about the purpose of education, yet such discussions are a prerequisite of reflective practice (Strauss, 2002:225). Professional discussions depend on colleagues talking to one another and trusting one another.

There are no definitive answers about what your values should be. Everyone is different and there is never total agreement within any group of professionals about what is really important. Work out whether your values are similar to, or different from, the lecturers talking about their professional values in the case studies below.

LECTURERS' SURVIVAL STRATEGIES

Focus on student progression:

Students come in quite naïve, with quite low self-esteem, low confidence levels, and the most rewarding thing is seeing my students go right through from Level 2 to Level 3 and now I'm doing job references for them. I think that's the ultimate. (Lecturer in travel and tourism)

College is a life-changing experience:

What I'm interested in is what they carry away. Some students carry away an enthusiasm, an interest in what you've done with them. That's a life-changing experience. You can't record that information. You can only know that from the smile when they say goodbye. (Lecturer in creative arts)

Students are more important than admin:

I think you've got to keep remembering what you're here for and try and spend time doing things that make things better for the students – not shuffling bits of paper. (Lecturer in performing arts)

The values expressed by these lecturers depict certain tensions between:

- concern for students' progression versus expectations of college management;
- education as life-enhancing versus instrumental to get a qualification;
- dealing with students versus dealing with paperwork.

These values arise from the lecturers' own experiences. If you suspect your values are oppositional to those held by others, you may feel as if you are not on the same wavelength as they are, and this can be demoralizing. Elliott (1991) urges us not to equate resistance to new policies or management directives with oppositional behaviour. Elliott rejects the idea that resistance to management expectations and organizational procedures must be in forms of rebellion and obstruction. He advocates 'creative conformity', which is a way of complying with policy and the prevailing organizational culture but in a creative way, that is though novel interpretations of policy. In this way he suggests you can transform the way you work by incorporating your values and constructing worthwhile experiences, for example by seeing teaching as an *educational* process and enjoying interaction with students as learners while they are working towards their qualifications. You conform by reaching targets for achievement, but you do so by creative practice in the classroom.

Your job is more than producing quantifiable statistics for managers, inspectors and policy-makers. College managers are motivated by an increase in enrolment numbers and percentage pass rates, etc., whereas your rewards may be found in one student's achievement in overcoming disability or discrimination. For most FE lecturers, learning outcomes are not just the published syllabus criteria, but are to be found in students' personal growth.

If you are not in tune with changes that drive improvement in your college, Eisner (2004) suggests that you can generate other visions of education, other values to guide its realization, other assumptions on which a more generous concept of practice can be built. It is possible to accommodate your educational values *and* meet both the course criteria and college targets. It is if you compromise your values that you are likely to become stressed.

FOOD FOR THOUGHT

Keeping in mind Elliott's concept of 'creative conformity', reflect on Moore's (2000:14b) perspective on the significance of collaborating with colleagues in a way that:

... offers space for reflection and action, in which teachers can prioritise their own voices away from the direct shadow of central government's policies and directives.

A way to reconcile your values and organizational expectations is through your interpretation of the syllabus, and the creative way you plan teaching and learning. The task facing you is how to incorporate activities that enhance learner control into the study of your subject. Much has been written about the importance of learning to learn. In my view, the answer is not simply to introduce a course in study skills – although introductory exercises in an induction period are useful. Students cannot learn without content; you cannot separate the thought process from what you think about. My own experience is that transfer of study skills is a problem and so they are best acquired through studying your subject, as you have the understanding of the concepts and criteria inherent in it. How can you bridge the gap between what you know and what the students need to know? These 'Useful Ideas' may provide some strategies.

USEFUL IDEAS

Constructing a learning programme

1   **Start at the end**. Induction is a time to identify what students have to achieve to complete the course successfully, set goals, agree deadlines, clarify timetables and build positive relationships. Your scheme of work must incorporate gradual progression to achieve the goals.

2   **Be more concerned about what students do than what you do**. If you consider learner control as a goal, you have to organize teaching and learning that brings it about. You cannot just throw students in at the deep end and watch them sink or swim; you can't force students to be independent. However, you can foster the process towards independence by supporting them in facing the challenges of the course.

3   **Involve students in decisions about the course**. Discussing the quality of the sessions regularly and talking about what was helpful/unhelpful enables you to adjust the pace of sessions, be flexible about the sequence of topics, review learning goals and provide formative assessment.

4   **Work with the realities and unpredictability of teaching and learning**. Planning can go awry as you cope with interruptions, absences, latecomers and disruptions caused by bad weather. You may aim for continuity but timetable and staff changes outside your control can unsettle students. Physical conditions may be poor or ICLT and specialist resource provision may not be as good as you would wish. Students miss deadlines or fail to produce work. Students can fall out with each other or be disruptive.

---

5 **Don't try to cover every single thing in the syllabus in your sessions**. Plan to cover less in class, but in more depth, and actively engage the students with the content and/or materials. This is more motivating for students and encourages them to continue (or complete) a topic on their own outside class.

Yates (2004) advocates that an appropriate way for creating a learning environment at this time is to combine face-to-face teaching and learning with online learning, that is blended learning, which encourages learner control. A learning programme brings content and methods together. The next section provides an opportunity to examine ways of organizing sessions, once the overall planning of the learning programme is accomplished.

Organizing sessions

There is one more stage in creating a learning environment before the scheme you have planned is put into practice with students, and that is organizing sessions. No doubt you have a college lesson plan proforma to complete for each session. The pro forma will certainly require you to provide information to fulfil the criteria for inspection. There is a tendency for colleges to push for uniformity in aims, content and assessment yet, at the same time, urge lecturers to be flexible and creative in practice and able to respond to changing circumstances. My view is that you need to consider organizing sessions more broadly than just meeting the requirements for inspection. You need to incorporate your own educational values, as well as values that are highly regarded in your vocational workplace. The lesson plan is your servant – not your master. It must work for you. Tailor your lesson plans to your needs and your style. There is a lot of work and effort involved in organizing lessons so you need to be careful not to fall into the pitfalls that are highlighted in the following case study.

POTENTIAL PITFALLS

Jenny is in her second year as a lecturer in business and retail. She sets herself high standards but appears over-whelmed by her heavy workload. Jenny works long hours trying to get things ready, yet is often still unprepared for her lessons.

When I first started I was quite erratic. Some weeks I'd have a lot of stuff prepared and some weeks I didn't. So I always felt bad about what I hadn't done. Sometimes I'd be here about 9 o'clock at night and still think I hadn't got everything ready for tomorrow. The realization of just how long it takes to prepare a lesson dawned. I was getting very tired, so by Friday I was crawling up the corridor. You end up with exhaustion.

It's easy to end up exhausted like Jenny and feel guilty that you haven't always prepared for sessions as you would wish. But where do you start? There are so many things to think about when organizing lessons. How do you make it interesting without lecturing? How do you get the students to do more than you? The job of preparing a session plan can go on forever, so you have to draw a line somewhere.

The way you go about planning, preparation, classroom management and assessment of students' progress depends on the way that you perceive your role as a lecturer. As discussed in the last section, if you see learner control as a goal, then you are more of a resource for students. Your role is supporting them and providing opportunities to build knowledge – not being a dispenser of knowledge. Sometimes students may be more knowledgeable than you, and you need to value the experience they bring to the session. Managing teaching and learning needs careful thought in these situations, as the following case studies show.

LECTURERS' SURVIVAL STRATEGIES

Think of yourself as a scarce resource in a workshop:

You can only be in one place at a time in a workshop. So, when everyone is working on their own projects, I ask them to put their names on the board if they want to see me. I cross the names off as I see people and this gives me and the students a clear indicator of progress. Also, if I am really busy I can see at a glance if a student has already been seen that session. Putting the names up like this makes students think about what they really need to ask me and what they need to discuss with me. (Lecturer in IT)

Acknowledge students' superior technical knowledge:

Don't be threatened. Students are more aware of new technology. In the workplace they may be using the latest applications. You can use their workplace experience or prior knowledge. Get them to demonstrate the latest functions and share what they know with others. It helps both the student to develop presentational skills and me and the other students to gain up-to-date technical knowledge. (Lecturer in IT)

Thinking explicitly about your role in creating a learning environment is an important first step when organizing lessons.

CHECKOUT AND WORKOUT

There are many different models of teachers, just as there are many models of learners. If the nature of teaching and learning changes, how does the teacher have to change? What is their role? We have just examined your role as a resource for students, and I expect you are familiar with the notions of lecturer as facilitator, mentor, tutor or coach. Here are some more models for you to check out.

Teacher as co-constructor: Barth (2000) puts forward the notion that constructing knowledge is not a spontaneous act for students as learners. The teacher becomes the 'co-constructor' as he or she negotiates the meaning of knowledge with students.

Teacher–strategist: Moore (2000) proposes that, to take account of unexpected problems and challenges, teachers need to be flexible in their practice. This entails them working as a 'teacher-strategist', i.e. constructing strategies that draw on past experience but are firmly oriented to future practice.

Teacher as guide: Freeman (2003) describes the teacher not as a guru but as a guide – but does qualify this when he says a more accurate description might be of one who points out interesting phenomena occurring as a consequence of students' self-directed journeys. Dewey (1916) also imagines the teacher in the role of guide, but envisages them steering a boat. Dewey deems the energy that propels the boat must come from those who are learning, not the teacher who is steering it!

Teacher as artist: Eisner (2004) asserts that the highest accolade we can confer upon someone is to say they are an artist, whether as a carpenter, surgeon, cook, engineer, physicist or a teacher. Eisner argues that virtually all aspects of what we do as lecturers, from the design of the curricula to the practice of teaching, require the distinctive forms of thinking needed by artists to create artistically crafted work.

- Do any of these models match the way you think about your role as a lecturer?
- Can you describe in a word or phrase how you see your role as an FE lecturer?

The roles described above are different from the traditional notion of an FE lecturer. Instead of being on centre stage, the lecturer is now depicted as backstage – but orchestrating events and doing the directing.

It is evident that how you think of your role as lecturer influences the way you go about teaching and learning. I would claim that, far from being redundant, the lecturer's role is critical in creating a successful learning environment for students. The key point to bear in mind is that students are creators of learning rather than recipients of it, so it is a shared responsibility. Dewey makes it clear that the energy required for learning must come from students. It is not necessary to wear yourself out doing things that the students can benefit from doing themselves, for example using the Internet for research. However, a student can perform a task under your guidance that could not be achieved alone (Vygotsky, 1978). You support and question students about learning activities, and you create conditions for learning to occur. *You* bridge the gap between what is known and what can be known by the student – that is, create what Vygotsky calls a 'zone of proximal development' by the provision of support, which is called 'scaffolding'. In practical terms, a student can perform a task under a lecturer's guidance that could not be performed alone. The lecturer's role is critical, but what about the role of the student? What activities will make students want to learn and be receptive? The answer is to give students specific tasks to make sense of by themselves – rather than you telling them things. The tasks have to be structured, achievable and should incorporate a goal. Ideally they should be activities that hold the students' interest and that on completion are sources of satisfaction and success for them. The critical thing is that the students have to be actively involved and challenged to think for themselves.

USEFUL IDEAS

To get students thinking, they can:

- look at a diagram, photograph or picture and make sense of it;
- handle an artefact or tool and think how it was made, what it's for or where it came from;
- select appropriate definitions for particular concepts by comparing them;
- listen to two different sounds and categorize the differences/similarities.

Specific tasks, such as those described above, are not just to get the session started and the students to settle down. The purpose is to enable the students to use a concrete and relevant task that gets them thinking. The tasks cater for students who are visual, auditory or kinaesthetic learners. You must allow time to explain the task and for the students to absorb it. Then you need to spend some time on formative assessment through questions and answers, discussion or informal conversation. Students can then begin to:

- compare their new connections with other people's;
- rectify misunderstandings;
- verify what they found;
- generalize and link to course content.

Assessing learning is part of an ongoing process. If negotiation takes place, then mistakes are acceptable and they lead to analysis and reformulation of original ideas – that is, to formative assessment. In this approach, the lecturer is responsible for putting students in a position to construct knowledge. If you don't negotiate, you limit students' opportunity for higher order thinking. If you don't challenge them about how they came to their answers, or make them justify their remarks, you limit students' opportunities to acquire skills for independent learning.

USEFUL IDEAS

- Evaluate lessons and learn from them. Give yourself time to reflect on what you do: think about what you've done, how effectively it's working, and give yourself time to discuss it with other people.
- Give students time to think in sessions – don't answer your own questions.
- If a lesson doesn't go well, move on. Reflect on what happened and resolve not to do it again. Think positively and make an effort not to beat yourself up. Lecturers who dwell on negative events are the ones who get stressed.
- Student evaluations need not be just something anonymous at the end of the course. Make them a two-way

process and encourage dialogue *in* your sessions *about* your sessions.

- Swap roles with students in sessions, e.g. get them to prepare a case study of their workplace experiences; summarize a chapter in the textbook; do a mini-presentation of a particular skill; review a session; lead a seminar.
- Help students to diagnose their own performance and progress and suggest future targets. Check that the class activities bring about the outcomes you intend.

Dealing with classroom challenges

If you are being totally honest, most of you will admit to feeling vulnerable in certain teaching and learning situations. You may start the day feeling quite good about yourself and then a tactless remark by a colleague throws you. Perhaps your manager bumps into you and pesters you about something you haven't yet done, or a student who has been absent for a time turns up and appears to be spoiling for a fight. When you go off to teach later in the day, you're annoyed and on edge and, more than likely, you will take it out on students who arrive late for your session. If you do tackle them about lateness, a negative atmosphere builds up and there is friction in the class. You leave the session even more disgruntled, and by the end of the day wonder how you'll survive as an FE lecturer! Not only do you feel negative about the job, but you convey that to students and colleagues. Dealing with challenges involves working on your personal style, classroom organization, professional judgements and problem-solving skills. Barely a day goes by in an FE college without some challenge presenting itself, but if you are stressed and overloaded you may feel apprehensive about dealing with it.

If you are sufficiently at ease with yourself, you stand a better chance of functioning more effectively. You have to consider how you come across to your students. It is not a matter of appearance, dress or age, but the manner in which you respond to students and treat them. Look at some of the pitfalls FE lecturers identify below.

POTENTIAL PITFALLS

Kelvin is a lecturer in biology who is aware of challenges in his teaching:

I know when I haven't had a good lesson. I'm shorter. I'm impatient. It may be that you mistimed things; you are muddled even though you've planned things. You can't do this too much as you lose the group and things get worse.

Glen is a lecturer in sports, leisure and recreation and he reveals the challenge he found when taking on a new area of teaching:

I've been timetabled for classes in new subjects, when I was appointed for something completely different. I was asked to be involved in something new this year and it's been horrendous. I'm at my wit's end as to what to do. I just want to walk out of college sometimes because it's so difficult.

Tensions within groups are almost inevitable at some point, but if you confuse names, snap at students, make threats, forget important points or are unfamiliar with the content, your shortcomings are likely to be exploited by your students. It is not necessarily a lack of compassion, but students have expectations about how their lecturer should behave. Your personal style can contribute to a positive or negative learning environment.

CHECKOUT AND WORKOUT

On a scale of 1–5 how do you think your students would rate your personal style?

	Positive				Negative
	1	2	3	4	5
General attitude					
Personal mannerisms					
Voice level					
Appearance of confidence					
Amount of enthusiasm					
Ability to motivate					
Level of respect					
Communication skills					
Type of feedback					
Nature of support					
Clarity of explanations					
Suitability of questions					
Rapport with students					
Interaction with group					
Dealing with problems					

According to Rogers (2002), a positive personal style is thought to produce an environment conducive to learning. As a lecturer, you must be aware of the way you come across to students. Research suggests that an FE lecturer's disposition – that is their personal nature, temperament, outlook and actions – are a major influence on students' learning (Hodkinson and James, 2003). Therefore it is important to ensure that what comes across is what you *intend*, and that it reflects your educational values.

You need not only to work out how your students react to your sessions, but you also have to look at your response to them. Does your reaction to an incident make it worse and sustain it rather than solve it? To work towards creating a more positive learning environment, you may have to modify your personal response to students. Self-examination of this kind is not intended to make you feel inadequate. If you always feel bad about yourself there is a tendency to rationalize your actions rather than learn from them. Teaching and learning doesn't always have to be about crisis management. If you show you are interested in the ideas that students are currently exploring, and assist them in making sense of things, then you build a positive environment. Helping students express aspirations and enthusiasm as well as doubts and fears contributes to this.

FOOD FOR THOUGHT

- Can you identify positive moments from your sessions that contributed to creating a learning environment?
- Can you identify how you put your personal stamp on teaching and learning to render it effective?

Presentations and whole group work can engage students' attention and convey relevant information, but need to be complemented with activities that allow for student variation and differences. Getting the pace of the class right is a problem: one student is likely to say you go too quickly while another thinks the class is too slow. To enable students to work more at their own pace, rather than yours, means breaking the class into sub-groups. The dynamics of the group, for example different expectations, friendship patterns and behaviour, affect how sub-groups work together. Key individuals – whether they are leaders, stars or isolates – can make or mar conditions for learning and discourage cooperation. Students are not always openly hostile and undercurrents are sometimes difficult to detect. If you have prepared well you are likely to be more successful, but you will still need to deal with the unpredictability of the classroom. Try and involve students in running the classroom activities and organizing learning activities. Getting students to work with those outside their friendship groups is often difficult, but you could think about getting them to form groups according to their star signs, month of birth, beginning letter of name, learning style, etc. If your aim is for students to work cooperatively, you must provide opportunities for this.

At the start of a course, you need to be specific about your expectations, and develop a rapport with students to identify their expectations. Learning agreements are usually completed by students at the beginning of a course, but these do not usually deal with expectations of everyday classroom behaviour and routines. If you negotiate a clear code, which can form a framework for working in your sessions, then you start the discussion about what it means to be a member of a particular learning or vocational community. Here are some ideas for such a code that FE lecturers use:

- Turn up to sessions on time.
- Bring the necessary equipment/materials to each session.
- Complete assigned tasks by the agreed deadline.
- Complete work between sessions as required.
- Be prepared to participate in activities.
- Take responsibility for your own progress.
- Respect each other.
- Safety rules are to be followed at all times.
- Finish work and clear away on time, not well before time.

These guidelines incorporate basic considerations for other people, and provide ideas about what is appropriate for you and your students. The important thing is to negotiate protocols with each group – rather than impose them ready-made. According to their level and ability, this activity can be more or less sophisticated. Students studying business management might engage in discussions of the ethics of protocol setting, whereas school students on vocational training courses may need practical guidelines about classroom routine. If appropriate, get the students to prepare a wall-chart for display in the room or a handout for everyone. If you do not make the protocols explicit, they remain a hidden agenda and can be a constant source of disagreement and heated discussion during the course. When the protocols are negotiated by a group, my experience is that they gradually use them to monitor each other's behaviour – you don't have to remind them constantly or reprimand them.

It is all too easy to make snap decisions and assumptions about students' behaviour. You arrive at class keen to present a carefully prepared session, and the class appears unwilling to participate. Realistically, you cannot expect everyone to be attentive and interested all the time, but when students appear indifferent it is difficult not to get impatient. You have to remember that students' behaviour at any given time is dominated by those needs which are immediate. Move around the class and observe what is going on. Be aware when the students' attention is drifting. However hard you try, there are occasions when your attempts to motivate students fail. If their expectations are not met, or students see little point in the lesson, they become bored and turn to others in the group as a source of interest, entertainment and amusement. This disruption probably annoys both you and their peers. Some students are prone to emotional outbursts in sessions. There could be many reasons for this: attention-seeking; lack of self-esteem; fear of failure; lack of motivation; negative opinion of themselves; negative emotions about college; or because they can't understand the work.

Whatever the reasons, you have to deal with the outbursts because they impinge on other students' learning. Talking to individual students about their behaviour, preferably in one-to-one tutorials later, is a step to helping them adjust to college life. Don't try and tackle these issues in class, or when emotions are intense.

USEFUL IDEAS

- Analyse why you feel uncomfortable with the student's behaviour. If you find it unacceptable it is likely that others will too, but don't humiliate the student in front of his or her peers. Don't tell students to grow up and then treat them like children!

- Controlling students' behaviour is not done to assert your personal authority, but to enable them to work towards a situation in which *they* control it more and *you* control it less. Your role is to initiate students into the process of assuming responsibility for their own behaviour, and participating sensibly in sessions.

- Although it is difficult, try to be calm and factual in your response. Tell the student disrupting the class or harassing another student that you cannot work in such circumstances.
- You indicate that you have the problem – not them – so the emotional temperature is less likely to rise. This gives students a chance to stop or apologize. If the student didn't deliberately set out to confront you, or didn't realize how disruptive their behaviour was, they will probably stop and say sorry. Don't cut the student off abruptly when they are offering an excuse, or explaining their behaviour. Give them a chance and hear them out.
- If the student doesn't respond, take control of the situation. You can listen but you must also confront, it is not a matter of either/or. If they start to argue, say something like: 'Fine – but that is not the way it is going to be.'
- Don't assert authority by standing up in front of the class and disciplining everyone but ask the disruptive student to wait outside the classroom door so that you can get the group back on task.
- Speak to the disruptive student when they are on their own in the corridor. You can ascertain what caused the outburst and deal with it one to one. Be clear what is to happen next. The group don't hear what you say, so it is effective if the student comes in and resumes work in a reasonable manner.
- Tell the group what has happened, so there are not opportunities for further disruption. Tell them this sort of thing makes you uptight and is not an acceptable way of working, and try and carry on as normal.
- If the student's behaviour is a threat to the safety of others, then tell the group to take a break and leave the room. Isolate the student and get help because you cannot deal with sudden outbursts of rage or violence on your own.

In my experience, serious behavioural challenges are not encountered that often. What you are likely to have to deal with more often as an FE lecturer is low-level disruption to lessons – backchat, rudeness, calling out – that makes teaching and learning more difficult. More often than not, conflict in the classroom arises out of a student's thoughtlessness, such as speaking out of turn, or their carelessness, such as forgetting work, losing things and breaking equipment. Disruption is often a result of students bringing fun into working in class. You know how far to go and when to stop – but students often don't. It is your professional judgement as to what is appropriate in college. Students often say that swearing and practical jokes are acceptable in the workplace, but in college you have a responsibility to address issues of equity and discrimination.

Colleagues may give you advice, but in the end you have to work out how to respond to a full range of classroom challenges. If work in class is being held up by one person, you have to be sensitive both to that individual's needs and the group's needs. Your professional judgement involves knowing when to bend the rules and when to stick to the rules hard and fast. You have to set the boundaries and persuade the students to comply.

Challenges in class don't always arise out of verbal clashes. Students are often sensitive about written feedback and demand an explanation of what you have written about their work. Marking can create problems, as the following case study reveals.

POTENTIAL PITFALLS

Brenda is a lecturer in hairdressing who assesses students in college and in the workplace:

When I started there were several occasions where I felt very, very overwhelmed with marking. Obviously, I was a novice at marking and all these assignments were just piled up. Great big portfolios all round my desk, and I just burst into tears.

As Brenda soon found out, marking is demanding for lecturers and requires skills and confidence. It is not just the volume of marking that is a cause for concern but, more often than not, your marking is subjected to a form of internal verification. The worry is whether you have given the correct grade and been consistent, or whether your colleagues will be critical of what you have done. Marking is taxing, requires professional judgement and is very often done to a strict deadline, which all create pressure.

USEFUL IDEAS

- Ensure that the students know what is required before they complete the assignment.
- Mark the piece of work – not the student. By that I mean don't write 'you did this or that' but 'the assignment covers this criteria and this is demonstrated by . . .'.
- Address the learning outcomes or criteria specifically.
- Be positive about what the assignment contains, but address what is missing also.
- Give advice about how the student can improve their work in future.
- Don't think of verification processes as a threat, but as an opportunity to learn from more experienced colleagues.
- Be sensible about how long marking takes and negotiate realistic return dates.

FOOD FOR THOUGHT

Creating a learning environment is a challenge for any lecturer. Sometimes you get instant rewards from listening to the buzz of activity in the session, and receiving positive feedback from students. More often than not you don't get this immediate feedback, despite your efforts to create a positive learning environment. To survive, you need to remember that teaching is a long-term investment and it may not be until many years later that a student realizes the effectiveness of your sessions. Don't be despondent but consider this:

> All we can say about the educational value of an experience is: we'll have to wait and see. (Biott, 2002:54)

Remember, learning is a continuous process and, for students, future events will alter the significance of what took place during college sessions.

6 Interpreting your role

In this chapter, I bring together the themes introduced in the previous chapters and reiterate their importance for surviving in the FE sector. Lecturers who survive best manage workloads effectively, use workplace experience constructively, develop positive relationships and create an environment conducive to their students' learning. The assumption that these strategies are significant for survival in FE is maintained throughout the *Survival Guide*. However, if you adopt these strategies, can I guarantee that they will work for you? You may want to be told exactly what to do, to know what the answers are or what the secret is. Despite repeated experiences in life to the contrary, many of us persist in looking for one answer, the quick fix, or the ultimate solution that will solve all problems (Brookfield, 1991). Unfortunately, it is not as simple as that!

If you imagine these strategies as strands that form a net or mesh, there appear to be other more obscure, and sometimes hidden, factors that unite them, which are like knots in the net. These knots bring into being a unifying framework that enables lecturers to employ the strategies effectively. If the knots are strong then the net holds things together. If they are weak then the net is strained or breaks and things fall apart. Two of the sometimes hidden factors that underpin effective employment of the strategies appear to be a lecturer's clarity of purpose, and a tendency to look to the future. These are the key issues that I discuss in this chapter, and they are ones that influence your ability to survive in FE.

You can deliberate on the values you bring to your role as an FE lecturer and why you came into the sector in the first place and identify your vision and purpose, but you cannot accurately predict *future developments* in the FE sector. However, you can speculate about them, because the future never represents a clean break with the past (Denzin and Lincoln, 1998). When you consider implications for your survival, you have to bear in mind that you do so with reference to the present, and with knowledge of the past. You can't plan for the future from a blank sheet but have to start from the current situation in the FE sector – good or bad. You have to take into account past actions – whether they failed or were successful – and identify what meaning you can take from past experiences that will enable you to survive in the future. It is what you learn from your review of the past, and the meaning you give to your current experiences, that has a bearing on your future actions. This involves paying attention to constraints as well as possibilities: that is, being aware of the details of what you do, your daily routine, what you think and feel. In this way you can start constructing a net as a structure within which you can create a climate for exploring personal meanings, and the influence of others in your college and in the FE sector, on your survival strategies.

Clarity of purpose

Any serious attempt to improve the effectiveness of your role must start from an understanding of what people in classrooms do at present, and be informed by an understanding of how experienced lecturers do their work (Cooper and McIntyre, 1996). 'Potential Pitfalls' are featured throughout the *Guide* and the case studies used give you an idea about the way in which some FE lecturers conceptualize their role, and attend to things that constrain them. The cases depict lecturers working to the limit of their capacity, of falling apart, and being thrown in at the deep end. These lecturers display behaviour that is not customary in the workplace, such as bursting into tears and losing their grip, which are symptoms of stress. Despite feeling inadequate and exhausted, they keep working and manage that stress in some way or another. That they remain in the workplace is a credit to their powers of survival – but it is achieved at a cost.

For many lecturers, working long hours results in constant tiredness. Even by working evenings, weekends and through holidays their preparation does not get done satisfactorily. Consequently, they suffer when they go to class feeling unprepared. In the classroom concentration can lapse and students respond negatively. This instant feedback reinforces feelings of inadequacy in lecturers, especially if they feel their efforts are not noticed by others or appreciated by them. One response is to blame themselves for mistiming activities and getting into a muddle when teaching or assessing. Another is to blame others, particularly students who are disruptive and difficult. Resentment builds up when managers expect administration to be completed, which takes time away from preparation for teaching or marking. Working conditions are also held responsible, for example pressures at the beginning and end of the academic year.

However, working harder does not improve things, as quality erodes when people are under pressure (Senge, 1990). Lecturers assume that, when these pressures ease, things will improve. But when you are stressed, feeling tired, trying to catch up and working against deadlines, the only way to survive is by lowering the quality of what you do. Administration, assessing and teaching all compete for time and attention, and lecturers feel their role is fragmenting as they switch from one job to another. They become casualties of the system as they spend time juggling competing demands, such as new procedures, curriculum changes, students' achievements and organizational problems.

What is not recognized is that there may well be more work to do than can be done to an acceptable standard in the time available. Lecturers who are stressed do not want to expose their weaknesses and may be reluctant to discuss these issues with college managers. Jameson and Hillier (2003) point out that college managers focus on six 'es'. The first three are efficiency, effectiveness and economy, routinely required in business. The second three are equal opportunities, e-learning and excellence in learning, and are quality processes required by government policies. What college managers appear to neglect is a seventh *e*, ethos: that is, the characteristic spirit of the college community and its systems. How lecturers feel and think about their college as a workplace, and the ethos created, is often assumed by managers. The hard truth is that you have to recognize that 'sometimes, no matter how hard an institution has tried to support staff through various initiatives, the generally cash-strapped nature of FE means that staff often feel very undervalued and overworked' (Jameson and Hillier, 2003:42). To survive, lecturers such as those depicted in 'Potential Pitfalls', make professional compromises, feel undervalued and overworked. They blame themselves for these shortcomings.

The reform agenda in the FE sector in England – driven through by a variety of agencies, quangos, sectoral organizations, examination bodies and government departments – includes a proliferation of new funding initiatives, quality assurance, audit, inspection and qualification regimes all jostling for implementation at the same time (Gleeson, 2005). Gleeson calls attention to the fact that the FE sector is far from well served by a balanced policy environment but, in spite of employer and government intervention, it reveals much real strength in FE teaching and learning provision. This resonates with the cases of 'Lecturers' Survival Strategies' used throughout the *Survival Guide* to illustrate practical ideas and advice about overcoming everyday problems encountered in college.

In contrast to lecturers who fail to avoid the potential pitfalls, lecturers who feature in 'Survival Strategies' focus on the possibilities their work offers. They still struggle with the reality of the FE college as a workplace, but set out intentionally to improve what they can. Their priority is on providing opportunities for students to achieve. Reflecting on the nature of students, the characteristics of good teaching and learning and evaluating critical incidents enable them to develop their own strategies and learn from new experiences (Vass, 1999). Making sense of practice through explicit acts of self-evaluation, for example regularly evaluating lesson plans, helps successful lecturers become more aware of experiences and able to use them as a source of learning – which is a valuable experience in itself and encourages continued learning.

The contrasting ways of working that feature in the case studies raise a question: why are some lecturers capable of overcoming workplace problems and others not? Not surprisingly, there is not one single, straightforward answer. One part of the answer may be found in a lecturer's individual differences and context. Another part of the answer may be found in a report providing guidelines for colleges on work-related stress (AoC, 2002). The report identifies that why individuals react to the demands of the workplace in the way they do depends on how they interpret or appraise the significance of a harmful, threatening or challenging event. How lecturers respond to workplace challenges depends on how they interpret their workplace experiences.

At some point, most lecturers experience feelings, such as those expressed by Moore (2000), of having let themselves or their students down in the classroom, and of questioning whether they will ever be as good a teacher as they would like to be. Moore suggests some may consider that classroom problems occur because of problems in their own lives, which stops them from devising more effective strategies. Although lecturers are urged to be reflective of their practice, and carry out evaluations of teaching in order to improve practice, my experience, which mirrors that of Moore, is that such reflections can lead to lecturers blaming themselves for workplace problems, because they reflect only on their own poor performance. This results in self-criticism, that is, thinking that 'something is wrong in me'. Others look beyond the classroom and consider the wider policies within which FE is sited and replace self-criticism with a more reasoned criticism, that is, 'something which is being done in the sector is wrong.'

Critical thinkers are aware that individual crises often reflect wider social changes, and make explicit the connections between the personal and political in their lives (Brookfield, 1991). You can't wish away the current emphasis in the FE sector on, for example, quality improvement, student numbers, funding and results, but you can use these as starting points to explore your workplace experiences more critically. When you are weighed down and encumbered by others' expectations, it is difficult to envisage that things could be different.

Another part of the answer to overcoming problems may be found in being aware of the details of your professional practice. This enables you to think about the way you construct your role as an FE lecturer. However, self-awareness in itself will not bring change; there also needs to be an intention to develop and the ability to behave in a different manner (Moon, 2000; 2004). This is clearly evidenced in lecturers' successful survival strategies, but is lacking in those who felt they had little control over their environment.

FE lecturers currently working in the sector are negotiating a shift in identity. They are confronted by new cohorts of students who require individual programmes and extra support in class, and are obliged to take on additional tasks such as quality assurance and marketing in the drive for colleges to remain competitive. Lecturers may interpret this as work overload and become stressed. The changing nature of the FE sector demands new roles: facilitator, tutor, assessor, verifier, invigilator, administrator, mentor, marketing, public relations. This may result in role overload. Working longer hours is a feasible strategy for dealing with work overload in the short term, but is an inappropriate strategy for dealing with role overload. This can be confusing if you have successfully employed working longer hours as a survival strategy in the past.

Role overload can be reduced by an agreed reassignment of role responsibilities. This has been put into effect by some college managers through the appointment of para-professionals, and the creation of posts with an array of different job titles: trainer, work-based assessor, key skills coordinator, section leader, progress tutor, advanced practitioner (Gleeson, 2005). These appointments reflect the increasing diversity and fragmentation of teaching and learning roles in the FE sector – and have not been universally welcomed.

When reassignment of role responsibilities does not happen, lecturers themselves tend to downgrade the importance of some of their roles to cope with role overload. Lecturers may withdraw from roles that managers consider important, such as administrator. Alternatively, they may spend more time on the administration and less time on their roles of programme planner and assessor. It is assumed that lecturers will recognize what roles to adopt, or drop, to be effective – even in a rapidly changing environment. Making a choice presents a dilemma, and what lecturers have to remember is that change is painful;

there are high costs in terms of self-image, insecurity, adjust-ment and so on (Minton, 2005). Such choices may be unset-tling, but out of such experiences come insight and more satisfactory lives (Brookfield, 1991). In some organizations the individual employee is expected to 'pick up' expected beha-viour, attitudes and skills. Hicks' (1999) research reveals that it is somehow expected that academics know what is expected of them in their teaching role, as a course leader or personal tutor. She likens the process to osmosis: while information or skills may be imparted quite explicitly in college, the values and attitudes will be implicitly communicated. Thus, developing clarity of purpose is left to individual lecturers.

When lecturers divide their work into teaching and non-teaching activities, then usually their perceptions are that non-teaching activities affect stress levels the most. Yet the paradox is that, although they are identified as non-teaching activities, activities such as recording of student profiles and tutorials, quality assurance documentation, course team meet-ings, organizing and evaluating work placements and planning and supervising educational visits are all *teaching-related activities* that have been bolted onto lecturers' workloads as educational practices change. However, when lecturers identify a distinct role for themselves as supporting learners, they tend not to distinguish between teaching and non-teaching activities. When all activities are undertaken to support learners and there is no real conflict; they have clarity of purpose (Steward, 2003).

CHECKOUT AND WORKOUT

Lecturers who are capable of overcoming problems, and who employ survival strategies effectively, have a clear idea of their purpose. One way to develop your survival skills is to create a framework identifying your purpose. The way you interpret your role is filtered and shaped by a con-ceptual framework that is largely implicit. The following questions should help you start thinking about what this conceptual framework might look like if it were explicit.

Your purpose

- What drew you to work in the FE sector originally?
- What purpose do you think your role serves?
- How does your role fit in with others in your college?
- How are you able to take control of what you do to achieve your purpose?
- What difference do you think your role as a lecturer makes to your students' lives?
- What particular qualities do you consider vital in your role?
- What keeps you going when things go wrong?
- What goals have you set yourself to achieve?
- What are you really trying to achieve?

I hope the questions have helped you to establish a clearer idea of what you want to achieve, how to achieve it and why it is important. When your conceptual framework is explicit, critical control of your role is possible. Your challenge is to construct a role that is consistent with your purpose, and yet responsive to the realities of your workload. What you have to bear in mind, as conditions in the FE sector are shifting, is not to be too rigid. As conditions change you have to be aware of better ones emerging and capitalize on them through what Dewey (1938) calls 'flexible purposing'. This way of thinking allows you to adjust your plan as things change without betraying your principles. Clarity of purpose must be congruent with current workplace conditions.

Looking to the future

In the last quarter of the twentieth century, Rogers (1983) described the qualities needed for individual survival in the twenty-first century. According to Rogers, writing all those years ago, the 'person of tomorrow' is keenly aware that the one certainty is change; that they are always in the process of changing. The 'person of tomorrow' is open to new experiences, to new ways of seeing, to new ideas and to unfamiliar concepts. What distinguishes them is that they are vitally alive in the way they face change and have self-   confidence and trust in their own judgement. We are in the twenty-first century now, so the 'person of tomorrow' is now the person of today. But are all FE lecturers vitally alive and self-confident?

The reality for many lecturers is pressures to be endured and limitations that must be accepted. If you define reality in this way, a vision of the future is an idle dream at best and a cynical delusion at worst – but not an achievable end (Senge, 1990). If you are constrained by an intolerable job you often cannot imagine other ways of working. While colleagues and managers might think it is in your best interest to change your ways, *you* must also want to change.

Eisner (2004) points out that, for artists, creating involves working within constraints. If artists just had to snap their fingers and their idea became a reality, there would be no creative process. The artist's task is to exploit the possibilities of a medium, and they have to learn to think within the demands imposed by the medium used in order to realize their aspirations. In the context of scarce resources in the FE sector, an outcome of the Transforming Learning Cultures in Further Education Project (Gleeson, 2005) recognizes that the practice of pedagogy is an art – the art of the possible. So the pertinent question to ask is: how do some lecturers achieve a view of workplace reality as a medium for creating, as the artist does, and work within its constraints, rather than view it as a source of limitation? Here are some ideas about what is possible in the future provided by lecturers currently working in the FE sector. The following examples show how they create their future role.

Ideas from Ancient Greece will still be applicable in the future:

Well, you could say you'll need to be IT literate and need the skills to develop a new curriculum. But I don't really think it's just that. I don't think what you'll need has changed since the Greeks. Students respond to a personality that's enthusiastic, someone who can explain things clearly and who takes an interest in their students' learning – regardless of who or what they are, or how difficult or awkward they might be, or what problems they have. I don't think that will ever change. If you add on that the teacher will need to be competent with the paperwork and planning – that's not what a teacher needs. That's what the awarding body says a teacher needs. But it's not the same. We all know as teachers it's about caring about students' learning – that's why we're here and that needs to be valued by the system.

Daily work will still be a creative and collaborative process:

I think it will be very much like now. The college is built up every morning. It's created every morning from its staff and students. We share the process. It's a creative activity. It's nothing to do with rights or responsibilities. It's not about dividing things up; it's about everybody working together.

Adaptability and flexibility will be required to keep up to date:

To be effective in the future you have to be adaptable and flexible, and it is assumed you have the subject knowledge. You must be able to teach and put ideas across. I think you need computer skills. You must be able to use PowerPoint, produce high quality handouts and a range of resources. You must keep your data up-to-date. You must have access to up to date trade books and keep yourself up to date.

The role will be one of effective management of student-centred learning:

In the future there should be more of an idea of customer service – delivering the best. The future role will be different. The idea of the lecturer as a fount of knowledge will go. Subject expertise and enthusiasm will still be required, and more admin support so lecturers can concentrate on students and their learning. The lecturer will become a manager of the learning process. I don't think one can say we'll do it all online, because I don't think that's sensitive enough. 'Student-centred' means that it is right for that individual, and for some online learning is too isolating.

The above examples from lecturers about the role of the FE lecturer in the future reflect the values of those who provided them. They are based on the individual lecturer's past experiences and give the impression of wish-lists, that is, how current conditions could be maintained or improved. These lecturers don't seem to be looking too far ahead, or imaging radical technological changes, but they highlight fundamental aspects of the role such as subject knowledge, enthusiasm, teaching ability and student support. Their visions of the future feature personal skills and dispositions.

If you think of the role of lecturers today, there are ways of talking about the FE sector that could not have been foreseen or spoken about when Rogers (1980) was describing the 'person of tomorrow': incorporation, e-learning, the Learning and Skills Council, Foundation degrees, the Quality Improvement Agency, and Lifelong Learning UK. This brings home to you the many changes that have occurred over recent years, and how you cannot predict what may happen in the next 25 years. You don't know exactly what is ahead of you. According to Gleeson (2005), there is no blueprint for some unattainable future idealized state coming out of the Transforming Learning Cultures in FE Project. Rather, it is considered that what the FE sector needs is considerable 'agreement making' between everyone involved – students, lecturers, employers and policy-makers – about the future. However, what the lecturers' examples of the future display is a questioning of the validity of a future created for them by others, such as the suitability of online learning for all. They have created futures that reflect their own aspirations – just as artists do. They are at least partial authors of their own future.

To achieve this, it may help you to imagine alternative ways of working, question what you are being asked to do and analyse your underlying assumptions about your role as an FE lecturer. Such activities may be unsettling, but it is worth persisting because self-insight and a more satisfactory way of working can result. You don't have to welcome every new policy initiative with open arms, just because it is new. This is a time for reflection, and possibly scepticism, and a time to think about the arguments others present for change. Constant change, and the unpredictability of working in the FE sector, should not discourage you – despite the fact that certainty is often the very thing you long for! However, it is only an illusion. You can do nothing more than make best guesses about what will happen in the future. You can only speculate about it. You must still plan and organize for the future, but the planning may well be of a different nature. Systems and structures change, and inevitably your role changes. As your role evolves you become aware of new ways of thinking, new directions and new possibilities. You draw on past experiences but your thoughts and plans must be directed to future practice.

You can be realistic, and understand the demands and constraints of working in an FE college, and create your own unique future. Imagine alternative ways of working as you answer the questions below.

CHECKOUT AND WORKOUT

Your Vision of the Future

- What sort of future society do you envisage you want to live in?
- What are your aspirations in your role as an FE lecturer?
- What will the college of the future look like?
- What would your ideal future classroom/workshop contain?
- What will you do differently in your ideal world?
- What skills and personal attributes will you need as a consequence of doing things differently?

Once you start to look at current practice, and develop preferred scenarios for the future, you begin to question your role. You put into words your views on the type of FE sector you want to work in. The ability to change resides with the individual, as this lecturer explains: 'I think change comes about with individuals finding ways for themselves – not having changes imposed on them, not being told to do things differently – but being comfortable with change' (lecturer in hotel management).

There are always benefits and disadvantages to any course of action, and you have to get the balance right. What you do, and the way you change, must be a personal decision. There are some possibilities in the 'Useful Ideas' below.

USEFUL IDEAS

- You may not be able to achieve your ideal world, or the perfect conditions for teaching and learning now or in the future, but this does not mean that you cannot still maintain your ideals. You can still keep to your principles and maintain your standards and moral values.
- What will your curriculum vitae (CV) look like in say five or ten years' time? What are you doing today that will prepare you for your future? Think about it! Will your CV show development, and convey your enthusiasm for teaching and learning and your interest in the future? Remember, what you do currently is preparation for your future. Are you acquiring the necessary experience now to occupy your future role? Success is more than hard work or good luck, it benefits from looking to the future and planning action.
- There is scope for individuality and creativity in developing your practice, and there are alternative ways of addressing change that are still organizationally acceptable. You can create your own world within the college and still meet the expectations of students, managers, inspectors and examiners. What about publishing your ideas in your college newsletter or intranet – not to brag about what you have done, but to invite dialogue and ask if anyone else has done anything similar, as you'd be interested in sharing ideas?
- Setting time aside to undertake a formal qualification such as a Master's degree is an opportunity to develop your subject knowledge or expertise in teaching and learning. Stenhouse's (1975) view of the extended professional in education is of someone concerned to question and test theory in practice, as a basis for development. Studying with others is an opportunity to share ideas and demonstrate your commitment to professional development.
- Doing your own enquiry and research, e.g. through observation and keeping records accurately, will enable

you to build up a body of knowledge about how your students learn and how the needs of students can be better met. You might explore and experiment with ways of organizing sessions, and learn about teaching and learning in FE the way you learn about your own subject or discipline, i.e. through active involvement, practical experience and critical reflection. When you start to research your practice it provokes change, and it is challenging and motivating.

- Spend time in developing yourself, as well as resources, as it is the person in the role that makes it what it is. As teaching and learning become more interactive, communication skills and developing professional relationships become more important. Use information from evaluations and appraisals constructively to identify your strengths and weaknesses.

- Demonstrate your ability to your managers by taking on a wider role. There is a range of things you could become involved in: people management, financial management, marketing, public relations, community relations, project planning, IT support and development.

- To survive in the future you have to be ready to use your professional judgement and engage in 'agreement-making' with others in the FE sector.

Do these 'Useful Ideas' make sense to you? They are some of the things other lecturers have tried. Looking to the future is a creative process, as you don't know exactly what's going to happen or where things are going to lead. You don't know what new challenges are ahead. It takes a confident and secure lecturer to leave their 'comfort zone' and confront new, and as yet unknown, opportunities. Sometimes we make mistakes. But if we persist things seem easier – it is not that the nature of the task has changed, but that our ability to do it has increased. Looking around me today, it is clear those lecturers who hang on to past practices, and are nostalgic for old ways of working, are the lecturers who are struggling to survive. Openness to new ways of working is only possible if we let go of some of our old ways of thinking – otherwise we are just increasing our workload with every new policy initiative and curriculum change that appears.

In Chapter 1 it was seen that adjusting to a series of modernizing initiatives over recent years has presented a challenge for FE lecturers. I suggested in this chapter that a key to future success is a lecturer's clarity of purpose and tendency to look to the future. As you examine your purpose and future as an FE lecturer, Sir Andrew Foster's government-commissioned review of further education focuses attention on the primary purpose of the FE sector and raises fundamental questions about the future role of FE colleges (Foster, 2005). Issues raised by the reform agenda for the sector (DfES, 2005) address implications for the future status of the sector and its governance, structure and workforce. The good news is that the Learning and Skills Council (LSC, 2005) predicts more personalization of learning and a decluttered pattern of provision alongside more self-regulation of colleges. The bad news is that to achieve this they are getting rid of what they perceive as overlap, duplication, confusion and waste. Does all this have a familiar ring?

The sense of momentum is maintained as the Learning and Skills Development Agency (LSDA) evolves into two agencies: the Quality Improvement Agency for Lifelong Learning and the Learning and Skills Network. The Standards Unit (DfES, 2004) has set out plans for reforming initial teaching training within the Learning and Skills sector in order to equip teachers with the skills they need to teach in the future. Lifelong Learning UK (LLUK) is developing standards and specifications across the sector. From 2007, those enrolling as trainees will register with the Institute for Learning (IfL) and there will be two stages leading to Qualified Teacher Learning and Skills status (QTLS): an initial 'passport to teaching' module and full qualification. The IfL will register those who successfully complete the two stages as holding a full licence to practise. The reforms not only affect new lecturers, but also experienced lecturers, as everyone needs to renew their licence on a regular basis by completing an annual tariff of appropriate continuing professional development options.

All these initiatives are indicators that you can be certain of one thing only – the future will bring change! How you make sense of it will either be empowering or disempowering. As Sir Andrew Foster deliberates on the purpose and future of the FE sector, he points out that there is a gaping chasm between the high value students place on their college education and the overall lack of esteem in which the FE sector is held by the wider community (Wilks, 2005). At least the students value what you do! Focusing on that fact may well be the best survival strategy you could employ.

FOOD FOR THOUGHT

To summarize my thoughts about surviving in FE, Bruner's (1997) tenet on self-esteem is an apposite note to finish on:

> The management of self-esteem is never simple and never settled, and its state is affected powerfully by the availability of supports provided from outside. These supports are hardly mysterious or exotic. They include such homely resorts as a second chance, honour for a good if unsuccessful try, but above all the chance for discourse that permits one to find out why, or how, things didn't work out as planned.

Bruner suggests that our self-esteem is powerfully affected by the chance for discourse to find out why things didn't work out as planned. In Foster's view the most important aspects that didn't work out as planned in the FE sector are how funding is managed, how priorities are established and what the rationale is for them. I would suggest that these are for policy-makers and college managers to attend to. Your toolkit of survival strategies, which you need to employ everyday, must contain discourse with colleagues about how to solve problems that you all face collaboratively and conversations with students about their learning. Challenges are still coming from several quarters. To survive in FE means you have to be open to new experiences and new ideas and accept that you are always in the process of change.

References

Argyle, M. (2001) *The Psychology of Happiness*. London: Routledge.

Armitage, A., Bryant, R., Dunnill, R., Hayes, D. and Renwick, M. (2003) *Teaching and Training in Post-Compulsory Education* (2nd edn). Buckingham: Open University Press.

Ashcroft, K. and James, D. (eds) (1998) *The Creative Professional: Learning to teach 14–19 year olds*. London: Falmer.

Association of Colleges Joint Working Party (AoC) (2002) *Work-related Stress: Joint guidance for colleges*. London: AoC.

Avis, J. (1999) 'Shifting identity: new conditions and the transformation of practice – teaching within post-compulsory education', *Journal of Vocational Education and Training*, 51(2), 245–64.

Avis, J., Bathmaker, A. and Parsons, J. (2001) 'Reflecting on method: the use of a time-log diary to examine the labour process in further education lecturers', *Research in Post-Compulsory Education*, 6(1), 5–18.

Barth, B.-M. (2000) 'The teachers' construction of knowledge', in B. Moon, J. Butcher and E. Bird (eds) *Leading Professional Development in Education*. London: RoutledgeFalmer.

Biott, C. (2002) 'Latency in action research: changing perspectives on occupational and researcher identities', in C. Day, J. Elliott, B. Somekh and R. Winter (eds) *Theory and Practice in Action Research*. Wallingford: Symposium Books.

Bolton, G. (2001) *Reflective Practice: Writing and professional development*. London: Paul Chapman.

Brookfield, S. (1991) *Developing Critical Thinkers: Challenging adults to explore alternative ways of thinking and acting*. San Francisco, CA: Jossey Bass/Wiley.

Bruner, J. (1997) *The Culture of Education*. Cambridge MA: Harvard University Press.

Clow, R. (2005) 'Just teachers: the work carried out by full-time further education teachers', *Research in Post-Compulsory Education*, 10(1), 63–81.

Colley, H., James, D., Tedder, M. and Diment, K. (2003) 'Learning as becoming in vocational education and training: class, gender and the role of vocational habitus', *Journal of Vocational Education and Training*, 55(4), 471–97.

Cooper, P. and McIntyre, D. (1996) *Effective Teaching and Learning.* Buckingham: OUP.

Covey, S. (2004) *The 7 Habits of Highly Effective People.* New York: Free Press.

Cranton, P. (1996) *Professional Development as Transformative Learning: New perspectives for teachers of adults.* San Francisco, CA: Jossey Bass.

Curzon, L. (2003) *An Outline of Principles and Practice* (6th edn). London: Continuum.

Denzin, N. and Lincoln, Y, (eds) (1998) *The Landscape of Qualitative Research: Theories and Issues.* Thousand Oaks: Sage.

Department for Education and Employment (DfEE) (1998) *The Learning Age: A renaissance for new Britain.* London: HMSO.

Department for Education and Employment (DfEE) (1999) *Learning to Succeed.* London: HMSO.

Department for Education and Skills (2002) (DfES) *Success for All.* London: HMSO.

Department for Education and Skills (DfES) (2003) *The Future of Higher Education.* London: HMSO.

Department for Education and Skills (DfES) (2004) *14–19 Curriculum and Qualification Reform: Final report of the working group on 14–19 reform.* London: DfES.

Department for Education and Skills (DfES) (2005) *Education and Skills 14–19.* London: HMSO.

Dewey, J. (1916) *Democracy in Education.* New York: Macmillian
— (1938) *Experience and Education.* New York: Macmillan.

Eisner, E. (2004) 'What Can Education Learn from the Arts about the Practice of Education?' *International Journal of Education and the Arts*, 5(4), 1–12.

Ellington, H. (2000) 'How to become an excellent tertiary-level teacher: seven golden rules for university and college lecturers', *Journal of Further and Higher Education*, 24(3), 311–21.

Elliott, J. (1991) *Action Research for Educational Change.* Buckingham: Open University Press.

Fiddy, R. (2004) 'The vision for the HE faculty', *HE Issues: City College Norwich*, 4, Spring.

Freeman, J. (2003) 'Suffering from Certainty' *Research in Post-Compulsory Education*, 8(1), 39–52.

Foster, A. (2005) *Realising the Potential: A review of the future role of further education colleges* (www.dfes.gov.uk/furthereducation/fereview).

Gleeson, D. (2005) 'Learning for a change in further education', *Journal of Vocational Education and Training*, 57(2), 239–46.

Handy, C. (2005) *Understanding Organisations* (5th edn). Harmondsworth: Penguin.

Hanson, A. (1996) 'The search for a separate theory of adult learning: does anyone really need andragogy?' In R. Edwards, A. Hanson and P. Raggatt (eds) *Boundaries of Adult Learning*. London: Cassell.

Health and Safety Executive (HSE) (2005) *Tackling Stress: The management standards approach*. Sudbury: HSE Books.

Hicks, L. (1999) 'The nature of learning', in L. Mullins, *Management and Organisational Behaviour* (5th edn). Harlow: Financial Times/Pitman Publishing.

Hillier, Y. (2005) *Reflective Teaching in Further and Adult Education* (2nd edn). London: Continuum.

Hodkinson, P. and James, D. (2003) 'Introduction. Transforming learning cultures in further education', *Journal of Vocational Education and Training*, 55(4), 389–406.

Huddlestone, P. and Unwin, L. (2002) *Teaching and Learning in Further Education: Diversity and change* (2nd edn). London: RoutledgeFalmer

Jameson, J. and Hillier, Y. (2003) *Researching Post-compulsory Education*. London: Continuum.

Jephcote, M. and Abbott, I. (2005) 'Tinkering and tailoring: the reform of 14–19 education in England', *Journal of Vocational Education and Training*, 57(2), 181–202.

Kyriacou, C. (2000) *Stress-busting for Teachers*. Cheltenham: Stanley Thornes.

Lave, J. and Wenger, E. (1991) *Situated Learning*. Cambridge: Cambridge University Press.

Learning and Skills Council (LSC) (2005) *Agenda for change*. London: LSC.

Lumby, J. and Tomlinson, H. (2000) 'Principals speaking: managerialism and leadership in further education', *Research in Post-Compulsory Education*, 5(2), 139–51.

Martinez, P. and Maynard J. (2002) *Improving Colleges: Why courses and programmes improve or decline over time*. London: LSDA.

Minton, D. (2005) *Teaching Skills in Further and Adult Education* (3rd edn). London: Thomson.

Moon, J. (2000) *Reflection in Learning and Professional Development*. London: Kogan Page.

Moon, J. (2004) *A Handbook of Reflective and Experiential Learning: Theory and practice*. London: RoutledgeFalmer.

Moore, A. (2000) *Teaching and Learning: Pedagogy, curriculum and culture*. London: RoutledgeFalmer.

Mullins, L. (1999) *Management and Organisational Behaviour* (5th edn). Harlow: Financial Times/Pitman Publishing.

Oldroyd, D. and Hall, V. (1991) *Managing Staff Development*. London: Paul Chapman.

Peeke, G. (2000) *Issues in Continuing Professional Development: Towards a systematic framework*. London: LSDA.

Rapoport, R. (1999) 'Relinking life and work', in L. Mullins, *Management and Organisational Behaviour* (5th edn). Harlow: Financial Times/ Pitman Publishing.

Reece, I. and Walker, S. (2003) *Teaching, Training and Learning: A practical guide* (5th edn). Sunderland: BEP.

Rogers, A. (2002) *Teaching Adults* (3rd edn). Buckingham: Open University Press.

Rogers, C. (1980) *A Way of Being*. Boston: Houghton Mifflin.

— (1983) *Freedom to Learn for the 1980s*. Columbus, OH: Merrill.

Senge, P. (1990) *The Fifth Discipline: The art and practice of the learning organisation*. London: Random House.

Stenhouse, L. (1975) *An Introduction to Curriculum Research and Development*. London: Heinemann.

Steward, A. (2002) 'Invisible workloads: investigating lecturers' timetables in a college of further and higher education', *City College Norwich: The Research and Development Bulletin*, 1(3), 3–7.

Steward, A. (2003) 'Constructive practice: workloads, roles and continuing professional development for college lecturers', Anglia Polytechnic University, unpublished EdD thesis.

Steward, A. (2004) 'Developing a typology: A response to analysing disparate qualitative data', *City College Norwich: The Research and Development Bulletin*, 2(2), 37–40.

Strauss, P. (2002) 'No easy answers: the dilemmas and challenges of teacher research', in C. Day, J. Elliott, B. Somekh and R. Winter (eds) *Theory and Practice in Action Research*. Wallingford: Symposium Books.

Timperley, H. and Robinson, V. (2000) 'Workload and the professional culture of teachers', *Educational Management and Administration*, 28(1), 47–62.

Vass, R. (1999) 'Evidence based practice: self-awareness and management.' Paper presented to the Annual Conference of the Collaborative Action Research Network, University of East Anglia.

Vygotsky, L. (1978) *Mind in Society*. Cambridge, MA: Harvard University Press.

Yates, T. (2004) 'Using ICTL for teaching and learning: an emerging curricular model', *City College Norwich: The Research and Development Bulletin*, 2(2), 19–21.

Index